Femicide in War and Peace

This book discusses the phenomenon of femicide—the killing of women globally because of their gender—in peacetime and in war.

Femicide in war is different from femicide in peace, and yet the dividing line between the two is thin. Violence against women happens in many forms—from emotional, psychological, and financial abuse, and barriers to personal autonomy, to physical and sexual abuse terminating in murder. It includes infanticide, sex selection, misogynistic laws, and cultural practices, and can include genital mutilation, forced sterilization, or forced pregnancy. Women experience these forms of violence during peacetime, as well as in times of crisis, conflict, or national insecurity. The COVID-19 pandemic led to an increase in violence against women, as they were thrown back to their violent partners, who were released from jail because of the global plague.

This volume draws upon cases from both Global North and Global South to give a detailed view of crimes against women and how femicide is perceived in different countries. It brings together scholars from diverse countries and disciplines and from many parts of the world where femicide has never or rarely been reported. This book will be a beneficial read for advanced students and researchers of Gender Studies, War and Conflict Studies, and Terrorism. It was originally published in *Peace Review*.

Shalva Weil is a Senior Researcher at the Seymour Fox School of Education at the Hebrew University of Jerusalem, Israel, and Research Fellow in the Department of Biblical and Ancient Studies, UNISA (University of South Africa).

Femicide in War and Peace

Edited by
Shalva Weil

LONDON AND NEW YORK

First published 2023
by Routledge
4 Park Square, Milton Park, Abingdon, Oxon, OX14 4RN

and by Routledge
605 Third Avenue, New York, NY 10158

Routledge is an imprint of the Taylor & Francis Group, an informa business

Chapters 1–7, 9 and 10 © 2023 Taylor & Francis
Chapter 8 © 2022 Nwabisa Shai, Leane Ramsoomar and Naeemah Abrahams. Originally published as Open Access.

With the exception of Chapter 8, no part of this book may be reprinted or reproduced or utilised in any form or by any electronic, mechanical, or other means, now known or hereafter invented, including photocopying and recording, or in any information storage or retrieval system, without permission in writing from the publishers. For details on the rights for Chapter 8, please see the chapter's Open Access footnote.

Trademark notice: Product or corporate names may be trademarks or registered trademarks, and are used only for identification and explanation without intent to infringe.

British Library Cataloguing-in-Publication Data
A catalogue record for this book is available from the British Library

ISBN13: 978-1-032-48277-4 (hbk)
ISBN13: 978-1-032-48279-8 (pbk)
ISBN13: 978-1-003-38825-8 (ebk)

DOI: 10.4324/9781003388258

Typeset in Minion Pro
by codeMantra

Publisher's Note
The publisher accepts responsibility for any inconsistencies that may have arisen during the conversion of this book from journal articles to book chapters, namely the inclusion of journal terminology.

Disclaimer
Every effort has been made to contact copyright holders for their permission to reprint material in this book. The publishers would be grateful to hear from any copyright holder who is not here acknowledged and will undertake to rectify any errors or omissions in future editions of this book.

This book is dedicated to all the women, who have been murdered by men for no reason, except that they are women. In most cases, the women know the perpetrators of the crime. They are intimate partners or former partners, or family members in a minority of cases they are strangers.

Femicide can be eliminated, if only governments would allocate resources to deal with this heinous crime. In most countries in the world, as in the country in which I reside, Femicide Observatories are financed by private acts of philanthropy, and NGOs work tirelessly to combat this global plague. This book acknowledges the concentrated efforts of women and men, who work day and night in peacetime and in war, to combat femicide.

Shalva Weil
Jerusalem, Israel

Contents

Citation Information ix
Notes on Contributors xi

Introduction: Targeting Femicide in War and Peace 1
Shalva Weil

1 Socio-Legal Aspects of Sexual and Gender-Based Violence Survivors' Victimization in Kosovo 7
Jiří Němec

2 The Continuum of Human Insecurity for Women: Femicide in War and Peace 18
Laura Isabella Brunke and Tobias Debiel

3 Statistical Biases, Measurement Challenges, and Recommendations for Studying Patterns of Femicide in Conflict 30
Maria Gargiulo

4 Invisible Police Lethal Violence Against Black Women in the United States: An Intersectional Approach 44
Janice Joseph

5 Understanding and Addressing Femicide in Peacetime Zimbabwe 54
Kudakwashe Chirambwi

6 Femicide, Harmful Practices, Religious Organizations and the Law in the North Caucasus 71
Saida Sirazhudinova

7 Africa's Code of Honor and the Protection of Women 81
Komlan Agbedahin

8 Femicide Prevention Strategy Development Process: The South African Experience 94
Nwabisa Shai, Leane Ramsoomar and Naeemah Abrahams

9 Transitional Justice Interviews and Reflections: Perspectives of Women
  Survivors of the Rwandan Genocide Against the Tutsi on Reparation and Repair 112
  Noam Schimmel

10 Suicide, Femicide, and COVID-19 125
   Katerina Standish

   Index 135

Citation Information

The following chapters, except for chapter 10, were originally published in the journal *Peace Review*, volume 34, issue 2 (2022). Chapter 10 was originally published in volume 33, issue 1 (2021) of the same journal. When citing this material, please use the original page numbering for each article, as follows:

Chapter 1
Socio-Legal Aspects of Sexual and Gender-Based Violence Survivors' Victimization in Kosovo
Jiří Němec
Peace Review, volume 34, issue 2 (2022) pp. 140–150

Chapter 2
The Continuum of Human Insecurity for Women: Femicide in War and Peace
Laura Isabella Brunke and Tobias Debiel
Peace Review, volume 34, issue 2 (2022) pp. 151–162

Chapter 3
Statistical Biases, Measurement Challenges, and Recommendations for Studying Patterns of Femicide in Conflict
Mario Gargiulo
Peace Review, volume 34, issue 2 (2022) pp. 163–176

Chapter 4
Invisible Police Lethal Violence Against Black Women in the United States: An Intersectional Approach
Janice Joseph
Peace Review, volume 34, issue 2 (2022) pp. 177–186

Chapter 5
Understanding and Addressing Femicide in Peacetime Zimbabwe
Kudakwashe Chirambwi
Peace Review, volume 34, issue 2 (2022) pp. 187–203

Chapter 6
Femicide, Harmful Practices, Religious Organizations and the Law in the North Caucasus
Saida Sirazhudinova
Peace Review, volume 34, issue 2 (2022) pp. 204–213

Chapter 7
Africa's Code of Honour and the Protection of Women
Komlan Agbedahin
Peace Review, volume 34, issue 2 (2022) pp. 214–226

Chapter 8
Femicide Prevention Strategy Development Process: The South African Experience
Nwabisa Shai, Leane Ramsoomar and Naeemah Abrahams
Peace Review, volume 34, issue 2 (2022) pp. 227–245

Chapter 9
Transitional Justice Interview and Reflections: Perspectives of Women Survivors of the Rwandan Genocide Against the Tutsi on Reparation and Repair
Noam Schimmel
Peace Review, volume 34, issue 2 (2022) pp. 246–258

Chapter 10
Suicide, Femicide, and COVID-19
Katerina Standish
Peace Review, volume 33, issue 1 (2021) pp. 71–79

For any permission-related enquiries please visit:
http://www.tandfonline.com/page/help/permissions

Notes on Contributors

Naeemah Abrahams is the Director of the Gender & Health Research Unit of the South African Medical Research Council. She has worked in the area of gender-based violence research for more than 30 years. Her research focus is on the intersections between gender-based violence and health, including the interface with HIV and measurement of violence against women and children.

Komlan Agbedahin is a Research Associate in the Department of Sociology at Rhodes University, South Africa. He has worked with the United Nations in the Democratic Republic of Congo as Protection and Field Officer and in Haiti as Monitoring and Reporting Officer.

Laura Isabella Brunke is a Researcher at the Institute of Political Science at the University of Duisburg-Essen, Germany, and a Member of the Institute for Development and Peace. She specializes in the politics of human rights and gender in the Latin American region with a particular interest in domestic legal practice and public policy.

Kudakwashe Chirambwi is a Researcher and author in conflict, women networks, and violence, with a particular interest in the intersectionality of peace, security, and development. He is the Founder of the Peace, Leadership and Conflict Transformation Programme at the National University of Science and Technology, Zimbabwe.

Tobias Debiel is a Professor at the Institute for Development and Peace at the University Duisburg-Essen, Germany. His areas of research include crisis prevention as a leitmotif for development and foreign policy, global governance and world peace order, UN peace operations, state formation, and violent conflict and post-conflict state-building.

Maria Gargiulo is a Graduate Student in Sociology and Demography at the University of Oxford, UK, and a Member of Nuffield College, UK. Her research uses quantitative methods to bring clarity to human rights violations, especially in settings where data are incomplete.

Janice Joseph is a Distinguished Professor of the Criminal Justice Program at Stockton University, USA. She is presently the President of the World Society of Victimology (WSV). She is the Editor of the *Journal of Ethnicity in Criminal Justice*. Her research interests include gangs, youth violence, juvenile delinquency, violence against women, and women and criminal justice.

Jiří Němec is a Doctoral Student of Security and Strategic Studies at the Faculty of Social Studies at Masaryk University in Brno, Czech Republic. His work primarily focuses on the role of sexual and gender-based violence in conflict, reparation mechanisms for such violence, and post-conflict reconstruction in the post-Yugoslav area.

Leane Ramsoomar, PhD, is a Research Uptake Manager at the Gender & Health Research of the South African Medical Research Council. She has 18 years' experience in conducting quantitative research, impact evaluations, alcohol and other drug use surveillance, and desktop reviews in the areas of alcohol and other drug use, violence against women and girls, and their intersections.

Noam Schimmel is a Lecturer in International and Area Studies at the University of California, Berkeley, USA. He teaches a range of courses in global studies, African studies, development, and human rights.

Nwabisa Shai, PhD, is a Specialist Scientist at the Gender & Health Research Unit of the South African Medical Research Council. She has 23 years of experience working with GBV prevention interventions and researching gender relations, femininities, and women's experience of VAWG in cultural contexts.

Saida Sirazhudinova is an Associate Professor in Philosophy and Sociology at the Dagestan State University of National Economy (Department of Humanities Disciplines), Russia. She holds a PhD in Political Studies.

Katerina Standish is an Active Board Member of the Canadian Peace Research Association. Her areas of research expertise include peace education, hope curriculum, suicide, peace and conflict, and international curricular analysis.

Shalva Weil is a Senior Researcher at the Seymour Fox School of Education at the Hebrew University of Jerusalem, Israel, and Research Fellow in the Department of Biblical and Ancient Studies, UNISA (University of South Africa).

Introduction: Targeting Femicide in War and Peace

Shalva Weil

Femicide is the intentional murder of women because of their perceived gender and represents a female form of homicide. While most intentional homicide victims are male, the majority of intimate partner or family-related homicides are female. There are no up-to-date statistics on the extent of femicide globally, but in 2017, the UNODC (United Nations Office on Drugs and Crime) noted that one in seven homicides were femicides. A total of 87,000 women were intentionally killed in 2017, the most recent year for which statistics are available (UNODC, 2019). Of these, the vast majority of women – nearly 60,000 – were killed by intimate partners or husbands, former partners or family members. Femicide is a global pandemic but not recognized as such by governments or authorities. Until recently, the phenomenon appeared to be "invisible" (Weil, 2016), but in the last eight years or so, femicide has managed to attract the interest of NGOs and advocates. The subject of femicide in war and peace has never been studied.

Femicide in war is different from femicide in peace, and yet the dividing line between the two is thin. It is true that not every murder of a woman is femicide. Some murders of women may be accidental or even arbitrary. While most intentional homicide victims are male, the majority of homicides perpetrated in the domestic sphere are female. Femicide, moreover, is associated with patriarchal societies, which are characterized by male dominance and female subordination, but the murder of women because of their gender can occur in any society and in any social class. However, in peace and in war, the rules of the game change.

At the time of writing, a terrible battle is being waged in Ukraine. People are getting killed because of the megalomania of one man. As far as we understand, President Vladimir Putin does not want to kill off the Ukrainians: he is not aiming at genocide. He just wants Ukraine to belong to Russia: he is working out of a sense of entitlement to attain more territory, more land, and more power. In this war, it is men who are in control and men who largely being killed in armed conflict. But women are also the innocent victims of this conflict. Thousands of women have been killed or forced to leave their partners and become vulnerable to enemy armies. It may emerge at a later date that there was an attempt at systematic femicide, but meanwhile there are reports of sex trafficking, rape, and violence.

Violence against women exists in peacetime as well as during war. Violence can be viewed along a continuum of harm that includes everything from emotional abuse, psychological abuse, financial abuse, and barriers to personal autonomy and safety, to physical and sexual abuse, which sometimes terminates in death. Different definitions of the term "femicide" have included infanticide, sex selection, misogynistic laws and cultural practices, forced sterilization, forced pregnancy, and more. Women experience extreme forms of violence worldwide in periods of societal stability, as well as in times of crisis, conflict, or national insecurity. During the Covid-19 pandemic, violence increased globally with women thrown back to their violent partners, sometimes released from jail because of the pandemic; suicides also spiked (Standish and Weil, 2021).

In the past decade, research and advocacy in the field of femicide have accelerated after a long period of dormancy, and domestic violence is monitored not only for partner abuse but also with a knowledge that violence against women can end in femicide. As a result, femicide has become a significant global challenge of a new order. Broad definitions of the phenomenon have been offered to associate femicide with various social phenomena, including witchcraft, dowry marriages, feticide, genital female mutilation, and human trafficking (cf. Laurent, Platzer and Idomir, 2013). In general, the theme of femicide in conflict situations has tended to be avoided. However, the subject of the killing of women in war and peace is becoming more burning daily, as war does not appear to cease but continues unabated in places like Ethiopia, Afghanistan, and Ukraine. And peace sometimes is not quite peace, as societies are divided internally, with little agreement between different sectors of society.

For scientists gathered together in this volume from different academic disciplines and diverse countries, the challenge is to assess whether women are being murdered because they are women or because of their race, religion or ethnicity, or for all of these factors. It is up to us to decide whether women are killed because of their gender or because of underworld activities, or serious conflicts which pull families, communities, or societies in different directions. Among the Arab-Palestinian population in Israel, for example, which constitutes 21% of that country's total population, there has been a considerable rise in violence in recent years in the Arab sector (Weil, 2022), with 125 Israeli Arabs/Palestinians killed in 2021 in criminal acts perpetrated by warring families, but not arising directly from the Israel-Palestinian conflict. Most of the killings are homicides, but in 2021, 14 cases, or 11% of the murdered, were women or girls. It has been difficult to assess how many of these were the results of stray bullets or family vendettas, but only a small number were carried out as a result of dishonorable "honor killings" by family members or because of the fact that the victim was a woman.

This volume attempts to provide as broad a base as possible for a discussion of some of the thorny issues related to war and peace and what lies between them. The subject has never been covered hitherto in books or articles on femicide and represents a pioneering effort to understand the dynamics of the phenomenon in war and in peace. The contributors come from a variety of places in the world, including the Global South, and some of the chapters represent the first-ever reports on femicide in these countries.

This book opens with a description of femicide and crimes against women in the Republic of Kosovo, a country with a history of terrible war in southeastern Europe in 1998 and 1999, and only independent from Serbia from 2008 on, where men are socialized into what Jiri Nemec calls "toxic behavior" toward women from a young age. When they grow up and the men commit sexual and gender-based violence against women, the legal system casts' the survivors of gender-based violence back into a cycle of maltreatment. Socio-legal impunity is the norm for the female victims of domestic and other male violence. Kosovan society is characterized by social and religious conservativism, accenting values held dear in traditional communities, such as family honor, and patriarchal perceptions of sexual and gender-based violence and its survivors. Social consciousness concerning gender equality is gradually progressing, and slowly there is a move in the direction of strengthening human rights and acknowledging women's position within society, but, meanwhile, state and legal institutions still tend to minimize domestic crimes and femicides, thereby perpetuating the human security of survivors and threatening the future of potential victims.

As Laura Isabella Brunke has shown, the settlement of armed conflicts is normally accompanied by a significant decrease in collectively organized violence. However, many post-conflict and transition countries are still characterized by a lack of human security, as in Kosovo. Women are particularly affected by violent crimes, sometimes to a similar or even more severe degree than during a preceding war. Brunke grapples with the way human security for post-conflict and transition countries can be defined. Only recently has attention been drawn to femicides, and this is an important aspect of the transformation into a more stable society. The alarming situation in Latin America shows that femicides are taking place in many countries every few hours. Nevertheless, in recent years, social protest against gendered crimes is more prominent, and an awareness of human rights is increasing.

As Maria Gargiulo points out, data collection of femicide can be extremely trying, and at times even dangerous, since we need more data in order to understand the issues of violence and conflict mortality. To this day, in most countries, femicide statistics are part of homicide data, and this is part of the problem of the way the social order legitimizes or even tolerates the killings of women because of their gender (Russell and Harmes, 2001). As more types of data become available, such as digital trace data, the hope is that new statistical tools will be able to identify deficiencies in femicide registration and produce more reliable information on the killings of women and girls.

In the United States, there has been huge media coverage for Black Lives Matter, but very little realization that Black Women's Lives also Matter. So, although the United States is not officially at war, different sectors of society feel alienated from mainstream society. In an important article, Janice Joseph examines the nature and extent of lethal police violence against Black women in the United States, their vulnerability to police violence, and the responses in the media and elsewhere to their deaths. Joseph points out that, incredibly, Black women in the United States have been ignored in public discourse and in femicide counts.

As in many countries, in Zimbabwe the category femicide, or the killing of women because they are women, is subsumed under homicide, making it extremely difficult to interpret incremental trends of the murder of women. Kudakwashe Chirambwi carried out a cross-sectional study in eight provinces of Zimbabwe showing that femicide consists of intimate partner femicide, killings by family members, as well as political femicides and what Chirambwi calls "covert femicide." The consistent pattern that emerges is that men desire power, dominance, and control over women but that legislation is needed to recognize femicide as a distinct phenomenon.

This kind of control over women is exerted in the North Caucasus on the southwestern borders of Russia, which has a majority Muslim population. Here, Saida Sirazhudinova brings important and rare insights into femicides in the area, including "honor killings," as well as death as the result of female genital mutilation. It should be pointed out that currently, both men and women themselves approve of honor killings in order to sustain a family's reputation as they consider it important to preserve their society and follow their religion.

So what can be done to combat femicide in countries at war and living in the so-called harmony? An original de-colonial answer comes from Komlan Obgedahin that in Africa, we should aim at reinstating Africa's code of honor, the Ubuntu, in order to protect women in armed conflict and in peacetime. While international legal instruments, like conventions and treaties, are all valuable, the author suggests revitalizing the pre-colonial code of values of Ubuntu that would provide sufficient protection for women and have legitimation in African eyes.

A different, pragmatic answer comes from South Africa, a complex society where internal strife is still rampant and where the rate of femicide is high by any standards. Authors and practitioners Nwabisa Shai, Leane Ramsoomar, and Naeemah Abrahams have developed a femicide-specific prevention strategy using a phased, research-driven, and consultative approach.

A country-level definition of femicide has been refined, and five key strategic objectives have been prioritized: strengthening of legislation and policy; leadership and accountability; and building evidence and practice.

A discussion of femicide in peace and war raises the difficult question of the relationship between femicide and genocide. Femicide as a global genocide is an argument used and promoted by several prominent scholars, and particularly for a number of Latin American researchers and activists, the violent death of women is considered genocide. In addition, feticide, whereby a fetus is aborted in sex selection, has been regarded by some feminists as genocide: in India, it was estimated a decade ago that 50 million women have been killed or are missing. Contrary to this idea, it is pointed out that the concept of genocide includes a number of features like the systematic destruction of members of a racial, ethnic or religious group. Specifically mass killings, such as the Holocaust, or the Armenian genocide, where an attempt was made to wipe out a complete people, cannot be compared to femicide. Personally, I would argue strongly that femicide is not genocide, since women constitute half of the world's population and an ethnic minority or tribe is not targeted. Females do not constitute a genus, and a genus cannot continue without females.

Nevertheless, femicide and genocide are definitely connected. Today, in Tigray province in Ethiopia, a genocide is taking place. So far, 5–10% or 600,000 Tigrayans have been exterminated in war-related causes.[1] Women have been targeted for gang rape and brutalized sexually; some have been murdered because they are women. In 1994, a genocide took place in another part of Africa, in Rwanda. Over one million members of the Tutsi tribe were murdered, and tens of thousands of Hutus, who had rejected genocide and racism against Tutsis, were also massacred. Noam Schimmel gives us a rare glimpse into the voices of female survivors of that genocide by interviewing three women, who are today active in human rights advocacy for Rwandan genocide survivors. During the Rwandan genocide, Tutsi women were targeted for sexual violence on account of being both women and Tutsi. They experienced rape and deliberate infection of Tutsi women with HIV by Hutu genocidal militias with the explicit aim of causing them a tortuous death. The bodies of Tutsi women were mutilated during torture, thereby humiliating, devaluating, and dehumanizing women as women.

Given the incidence of femicide globally, which appears to be exacerbated during conflict, it is time to pay attention to its deleterious effects on all societies. This became even more evident during COVID-19, when women were confined to violent domestic spaces with abusive men, and rates of femicide,

---

[1] York, Geoffrey. 6 November, 2022. Recognize genocide in Ethiopia's Tigray region, experts urge Canadian committee. *The Globe and Mail*. region:https://www.theglobeandmail.com/world/article-recognize-genocide-in-ethiopias-tigray-region-experts-urge-canadian/

as well as suicide, rose globally. Femicide, like COVID-19, should be considered a pandemic (Weil, 2020). As Katerina Standish points out, societies have to face femicide and suicidal violence by combining medical and social models and tackling economic and social insecurity and aligning them with physical health. Prioritizing COVID-19 globally is legitimate, so long as other forms of violence, including femicide and suicide, which may be unintended outcomes of the pandemic, are treated similarly and prioritized too.

This volume on *Femicide in War and Peace*, then, brings forth new subjectmatter and new voices from diverse disciplines to the study of femicide globally. It touches upon lacunae in data collection, femicide definitions, and diverse attitudes to femicide in different countries, not necessarily associated with Western values. Beyond that, it requires readers to be sensitive to questions of legitimation, human rights, and redistributive justice.

REFERENCES

Laurent, Claire, Platzer, Michael & Idomir, Maria. (2013). *Femicide: A Global Issue That Demands Action*, 1. Vienna: ACUNS.

Russell, Diana E. H. & Harmes, Roberta. (2001). *Femicide in Global Perspective*. New York: Teachers College Press.

Standish, Katerina & Weil, Shalva. (2021) Gendered Pandemics: Suicide, Femicide and COVID-19. *Journal of Gender Studies*, 30 (7), 807–818. doi: 10.1080/09589236.2021.1880883

UNODC (United Nations Office on Drugs and Crime). (2019). *Global Study on Homicide 2019: Gender-Related Killing of Women and Girls*. https://www.unodc.org/documents/data-and-analysis/gsh/Booklet_5.pdf. Accessed 20 September 2021.

Weil, Shalva. (2016). Making Femicide Visible. *Current Sociology*, 64 (7), 1124–1137. doi: 10.1177/0011392115623602

Weil, Shalva. (2020) Two Global Pandemics: Femicide and COVID-19. *Trauma and Memory*, 8 (2), 110–112. doi: 10.12869/TM2020-2-03

Weil, Shalva. (2022). Femicide in Israel. In: P R Kumaraswamy (Ed.) The Palgrave International Handbook of Israel, Palgrave Macmillan, Singapore. https://link.springer.com/reference-workentry/10.1007/978-981-16-2717-0_50-1

Socio-Legal Aspects of Sexual and Gender-Based Violence Survivors' Victimization in Kosovo[1]

JIŘÍ NĚMEC

In Kosovo, violence against women is both a ground for and a result of socialized norms of victimization. Men socialize violent and toxic behavior toward women from a young age, and when they commit sexual and gender-based violence, victimizing norms are reinforced by the state structure during judicial processes, casting survivors back into the circle of maltreatment. Lack of conceptual understanding, violence relativization, and victim-blaming are components of structural violence perpetrated by the police, prosecutors, and judges when addressing sexual and gender-based offenses. Available research suggests that the majority of femicides are preceded by domestic abuse or intimate partner violence; thus, when gender-discriminatory norms are socialized both among people and institutions, and when socio-legal impunity is the norm, survivors of sexual and gender-based violence are exposed to an in-time developing spiral of violence. This spiral is determined by the constructivist relation of interdependence between agents – here individual people, the sum of whom constitutes society – and the state's structure – here the politico-legal institutions of the police, prosecution, and judiciary. Agents and structure, on the one hand, continuously reinforce the socialization of various types of violence against women within society, and on the other hand, they are only the ones who can interrupt the spiral. I argue that Kosovo's current state of affairs favors reinforcement over interruption.

Kosovar society is characterized by social and religious conservativism, accenting values perceived traditional in the community, such as family honor, and based on a historical tribalist legacy. Although social consciousness concerning gender equality is gradually progressing toward

---

[1] All references to Kosovo should be understood in terms of the United Nations Security Council Resolution 1244 (1999) and the International Court of Justice opinion on the Kosovo Declaration of Independence. This designation is without prejudice to the various positions on the status of this territory.

strengthening human rights and acknowledging women's position within society, the Republic of Kosovo, unfortunately, still suffers from a biased, one-sided, and predominantly patriarchal perception of sexual and gender-based violence (hereinafter SGBV) and its survivors. This social perception is projected, I argue, into various forms of structural violence perpetrated by the state against women in Kosovo, eroding their *human security* and, therefore, human rights. Sexual and gender-based violence is in this work understood in line with the definition articulated by the United Nations (2020, 6) and is used as an umbrella term incorporating conflict-related sexual violence, intimate partner violence, domestic violence, rape, sexual harassment, sexual exploitation, psychical violence, and various other types of gendered violence. Since this deliberation is not meant to contribute to the definitional or conceptual discussion, I do intentionally employ the term "SGBV" as an all-inclusive concept, endemic globally to both war and peacetime. Of the elements of SGBV, Conflict-Related Sexual Violence (hereinafter CRSV) is of vital importance for the case of Kosovo and will be particularly addressed in a dedicated section below.

In constructivist thought, individual states are understood as "agents" constructing the international "structure". In other words, the ways that agents behave in the international arena determines how the arena – the structure – works and behaves in backwards relation to agents. The relation between agents and the structure is mutually interdependent, i.e., agents and the structure constantly affect each other; however, such influence is hardly expected to change in the short term, and only extensive interference can reconstruct the nature of the interdependent relationship. Otherwise, change happens in an extremely longitudinal manner. Simply put, this means the relationship between agents and the structure is mainly repeatedly reinforced over time. In this work, I use the constructivist lens of interdependent relation on the level of interaction between people, understood as *agents*, and the state *structure*, understood as the politico-legal sphere.

Hence, I argue that people do have a constitutive effect on the structure of the state, its operational mechanisms and, vicariously, the exercise of its power (e.g., the police, prosecution, judiciary). Thus, when people socialize violent and toxic behavior toward women and normalize victimization within society, then the state structure reinforces these patterns via exercising its own politico-legal power. The repeatedly reinforcing relation produces a circle of violence toward women and when such a circle develops over time, it constructs an in-time evolving spiral. In line with this understanding of the interdependence between agents and the structure, such a spiral of violence is hard to break.

Society and the judiciary are the primary domains of interest in this essay. In the following pages, I strive to shed light on the structural violence perpetrated in the courtrooms, prosecutors' offices, and police stations in Kosovo against the survivors of sexual and gender-based violence. The SGBV-related law in Kosovo proves insufficient, and cases have occurred in which judicial omissions during SGBV-related trials led to continued physical abuses, sexual assaults, suicides, and eventually femicides. I argue that the entrenched patriarchal mentality of the politico-legal structure reinforces a structural victimizing approach and poses a direct threat to the human security of SGBV survivors by casting them back into the spiral of physical and mental violence.

WAR IN KOSOVO AS A BLUEPRINT FOR TACTICAL SEXUAL VIOLENCE AND A POOR STATE'S REPARATIONS RESPONSE

To understand the role, impact, and scale of the SGBV phenomenon in Kosovo, it is essential to refer to its formative history, which affects contemporary socio-cultural perceptions of violence against women in the country. Kosovo witnessed a substantial use of sexualized violence against women as a warring tactic, a systematic tool in the 1998–1999 war to attack the very fabric of the target society in order to dissolve it, and as a part of ethnic cleansing. However, the scale of such *tactical sexual violence* in the Kosovar conflict is a matter of ongoing discussion. Based on estimates by local non-governmental organizations that provide services for CRSV survivors, the number of persons affected by such violence ranges from 10,000 to 20,000 (Limanu and Marku 2014; c.f. Subotić and Zaharijević 2017, 239–264; Amnesty International 2017, 14–15). The latter number is widely repeated within the narratives of the Kosovar media.

According to the testimony of witnesses and survivors, the vast majority of tactical sexual violence during the Kosovo conflict was used by Serb paramilitary groups and police officers. However, revenge and retaliatory sexual assaults were also perpetrated by the Kosovo Liberation Army, especially in the immediate aftermath of the war, against the Serb population and other minority groups. During the war, the KLA used sexual violence against Kosovo Albanians suspected of collaborating with Serbs. Many of the testimonies confirm gang rapes, public rapes in front of family or community members, assaults, harassment, and sexual mutilations perpetrated by Serbs to dehumanize and dissolve the target Kosovo Albanian society. Serb propaganda and media narratives labeling

Kosovar women as "birth-machines" trying to overpopulate the Serbs in the region played a crucial role in the committing of these war crimes. Thus, women were seen as counter-value targets that needed to be addressed in combat, and accounts confirm that pregnant women were indeed subjected to merciless torture and femicides (for details, see OSCE 1999, Chapters 7 and 16).

Conflict-related sexual violence brings us to the very first legal aspect of SGBV socialized victimization in Kosovo, and that is the state's (mal)treatment of CRSV survivors. The initial "Law on the Status and the Rights of the Martyrs, Invalids, Veterans, Members of Kosovo Liberation Army, Civilian Victims of War and their Families" adopted in 2011 did not deal with the widespread sexualized war crimes at all. After the advocacy initiatives of civil society groups, the law was amended in 2014 to incorporate the *Sexual Violence Victims of War*. Undoubtedly, it was a positive step for many, but not for all CRSV survivors.

First of all, the law – determining eligibility and other conditions for survivors to apply for reparations for harms suffered – focuses only on the precise period of the war. Hence, only survivors of sexual abuse and rape that occurred between 27 February 1998 and 20 June 1999 can be considered *Sexual Violence Victims of War* (Assembly of the Republic of Kosovo 2014, 3), which means that survivors of retaliatory and revenge conflict-related sexual violence are entirely ignored and cannot apply for reparations. Considering that these revenge assaults were directed mainly against non-Kosovo Albanian ethnicities, the law constitutes a clear ethnic cleavage in the state's approach to the population.

Second, the law and two consecutive regulations designating procedures for verification and recognition of the *Sexual Violence Victim of War* status produced an environment in which women are forced to undergo interrogations by a verification commission and medical examination (both physical and mental) to be able to apply for CRSV reparations. Such an environment, naturally, catalyzes secondary victimization through enforced reactivation of memories of traumatizing events and places disproportionate pressure on survivors who often need to mask their reasons for traveling to committee hearings in order to conceal their experience from their families and communities. It is crucial to remember that Kosovar society relies on community principles, and sexual violence, especially in rural areas, is taboo. It is still common for women to be expelled from their families and communities to the margins of society after they confess to being sexually assaulted during the war, which constitutes a victim-blaming aspect of victimization. Hence, it is important to acknowledge that the reparations application process is stressful and traumatizing for survivors due to social pressures. The need for physical examination more than twenty years after these crimes were perpetrated is, to a certain extent, nonsensical from the medical point of view. It represents another humiliating threat to survivors' wellbeing, and the psychological examination, in a traditionalist society, contributes to the victim-oriented stigmatization as well.

Therefore, even though Kosovo is sometimes portrayed as a role model in addressing reparations for CRSV survivors (see Justice Rapid Response 2019), I argue that the reality is the other way around. The current reparations-related law exacerbates secondary victimization and falls short of adequate conceptualization of persons eligible for reparations by recognizing only a limited time period in which perpetrated war crimes are taken into consideration. Furthermore, there are five categories of internationally recognized reparations for CRSV survivors (for details, see UNGA 2005, 6–8), but the Kosovar state offers only a limited fraction of these measures, focusing mainly on financial compensation. To apply for reparations, the above-outlined process must be followed. However, medical treatments for conditions that are consequences of war and that are not provided or available for CRSV survivors within the Kosovar healthcare system must be sought abroad. Thus, as a post-conflict society, when Kosovo cannot offer such services, the state interferes with survivors' human security by constituting a *want* (for conceptualization, see Kerr 2007, 95) of both psychological and physical medical services. The extent of the use of reparations tools, once again, depends on the promulgated yet insufficient law which directs survivor women into a whirlwind of victimization, stigmatization, and structural violence.

MOVING FROM PAST TO PRESENT: WHEN VICTIMIZATION AND STIGMATIZATION ARE REINFORCED IN COURTROOMS AND POLICE STATIONS

One may suggest that extensive exposure to widespread conflict-related sexual violence, abuse, torture, and other war crimes would give rise to a deterrent element against the occurrence of SGBV in a society and catalyze advocacy, legal, educational, and reparations policies within the state. However, the empirical evidence suggests the contrary and gendered structural violence toward women – and survivors of SGBV in particular – seems to be entrenched in the Kosovar social and politico-legal sphere.

The World Health Organization (WHO) (2021) assesses several special factors of social behavior, understanding, and experience that affect the prevalence of *intimate partner violence* and *sexual violence* globally. Beliefs concerning family honor and male sexual entitlement, and weak legislation fall within a category of determinants specifically interconnected with the perpetration of sexual violence, and the category of determinants specifically interconnected with intimate partner violence – for example, marital dissatisfaction, male controlling behaviors, and one's personal history of exposure to violence. Concerning Kosovo, all of these specific factors are present in the social and politico-legal environment, followed by other, so-called risk factors such as, inter alia, lower levels of education, access to paid work and gender equality, social norms privileging men, harmful masculine behaviors, and witnessing family violence.

Firstly, from the social perspective, the research among Kosovar men indicates that a majority of the above factors are present in people's mindsets; men are raised in patriarchal families where women are ascribed kitchen- and childrearing-related tasks and subjected to sexual and gender-based violence. Twenty percent of Kosovar men witnessed intimate partner violence against their mother in adolescence and have incorporated this "problem-solving method" into behavior with their peers in schools and neighborhoods (OSCE Mission in Kosovo and UNFPA Kosovo 2018, 47). Based on the constructivist position, I argue that such learned behavior of *agents* is amassed and projected into the *structure*, co-creating structural socialized norms on the acceptability of SGBV. Furthermore, about twelve percent of men have slapped, hit with a fist, or thrown something at their female partner; thirty percent of men agreed entirely or somewhat that if a woman does not resist, sexual intercourse cannot be labeled as rape; and nineteen percent believed that women actually want to be raped. Finally, five percent admitted committing at least one non-consensual sexual act with a woman, and four percent admitted to forcing their intimate partner into having sex (OSCE Mission in Kosovo and UNFPA Kosovo 2018, 36–38). Hence, patterns of rape culture and victim-blaming (also influential in CRSV survivors' cases), aspects of secondary victimization, and the *specific* and *risk* factors mentioned above are prevalent in Kosovar society's approach toward women. In such a state of affairs, I argue, the *structure* as the sum of *agents* reinforces victimizing patterns that become socialized among these agents. This process is a cycle of structural violence, and as such, over time, constitutes a notional spiral.

Due to the under-representation of women in crucial structural positions, resulting in a lack of gender-specific experience in decision-making processes, victimizing patterns are also projected into the second aspect of this deliberation – the legal perspective. In Kosovo, state officials tend to lack a conceptual understanding of SGBV, confuse *gender* and *sex* with *women*, and misunderstand how gender relations contribute to structural violence against females. Officials' attitudes suggest that socialized gender norms may negatively affect their approach toward addressing SGBV – for example, by claiming that women wearing shorts "is a bad thing" or that people in Kosovo are not animals – and therefore it is unnecessary to address SGBV in the legislative process (Banjska et al. 2021, 56–59). Hence, although Kosovo amended its constitution to recognize the so-called Istanbul Convention, secured institutional support for shelters for victims of domestic violence, and broadened competence of the police in this area, all in 2020, the execution of these advancements often falls short. It seems it is especially the police, prosecution, and judiciary that manifests noted socialized gender norms in courtrooms and police stations, thereby catalyzing secondary victimization and structural violence.

In SGBV-related cases, courts often hand down the most minimal sentences prescribed by the criminal code of Kosovo. Protection orders in response to victims' requests are ordinarily delayed; verification periods are of minimal length; judges often defend such rulings with words like "the court considers the sentence fair"; and appeals courts tend to reduce or completely reverse the sentences of SGBV perpetrators (EULEX 2020, 29; cf. OSAC 2020). Since evidence indicates that up to seventy percent of femicide victims were previously subjected to intimate partner and domestic violence committed by the same perpetrator (Campbell et al. 2003, 1091; cf. Carey and Torres 2010, 142–163; Hernández 2021; WHO 2012), we may deduce that reducing sentences and downplaying the gravity of SGBV cases not only perpetrates structural violence and poses a *want* of expected justice, but also exposes survivors to the threat of eventual femicide. According to Kosovo police reports, domestic and intimate partner violence rose by about sixty percent in the 2014–2019 period; violence was directed against women in about eighty percent of incidents every year, and cases are likely underreported due to the perception of SGBV as a personal matter between partners or families (Agency for Gender Equality of Kosovo 2020, 1). The novel coronavirus pandemic is also expected to aggravate sexual and gender-based violence cases.

An illustration of socially entrenched victimizing norms and a reductionist approach to SGBV can be found in particular cases. Civic monitors of SGBV-related court proceedings reported that judges often try to reconcile the victim and the perpetrator instead of issuing rulings and imposing punishments according to the law, claiming the parties should patch up for the sake of the family or children. Reports cite judges who rejected the protection order application of a female party to the hearing, who was prevented by the perpetrator from seeing her children, because the judge concluded she still loved the accused. There are judges who claim that the goal of punishing SGBV offenders is to bring the family back together, not to ruin the relationship of wife and husband (Banjska et al. 2021,

93–99). Sentences are reduced not only in non-lethal SGBV cases but also in aggravated femicides. That means excessive violence with force exceeding that necessary to terminate a life, or torture preceding death occurred during the killing. In 2021 a life imprisonment prescribed by the criminal code for aggravated murder was reduced to twenty-four years for a man who has beaten his wife to death with a metal rod and then killed their nine-year-old daughter (Kosovo Women's Network 2020). In early 2021, a man murdered his ex-wife after her daughter reported the mother was physically abused by her ex-husband, who had already been reported for abuse in 2019. The state prosecutor failed to pursue the case, and allegedly downplayed the report because the victim herself did not report the crime, and claimed the victim did not want to prosecute since she did not come to her second questioning about the case (Bami 2021). Another institutional failure occurred in early 2022 when femicide was committed with a gun after the victim reported psychological abuse from her intimate partner. The police failed to issue a protection order and released the suspect in due course following the prosecutor's order (Bami 2022). Possession of a gun (common in Kosovo, be it legal possession or not) is another risk factor catalyzing SGBV toward femicide (Campbell et al. 2003, 1090). Other grave instances of SGBV in Kosovo include the rape of a minor girl by a teacher; rape of a minor girl by a policeman and his accomplice; and a two-day-long continued sexual assault resulting in femicide of an eighteen-year-old woman left to die in front of a hospital entrance by perpetrators with substantial criminal records.

As an early constructivist, Michael Foucault, notes, the state's perception of the gravity of a crime is mirrored in the way its courts decide on a punishment (Carey and Torres 2020, 150). Thus, in Kosovo, the state's approach is materialized in noncommittal court rulings, judges trivializing SGBV incidents, and forced reconciliations. All of these issues further reflect the blindness of the state structure to perpetrators' previous intentions to do harm and their socialized patriarchal entitlement and dominance (Dekel and Andipatin 2016), and to the use, or threat of use, of weapons – known risk factors directly connected to femicide (Hernández 2021). Thus, although the phenomenon of femicide is an extreme manifestation of SGBV, the above-described matrix of socio-legal impunity is intrinsic to Kosovo and contributes to the escalation of violence, even to the most severe forms.

CONCLUSION: THE UNBREAKABLE RELATION OF AGENTS AND STRUCTURE?

In this piece, I aimed to demonstrate with practical evidence of sexual and gender-based violence that Kosovo flounders in a continued spiral of a victimizing approach to its women. I argued that gendered attitudes socialized in society – the sum of its constitutive agents – shape the execution of politico-legal power and, vice versa, that gender-discriminatory execution of power in police stations, prosecutors' offices, and courtrooms contributes to the socialization of victimizing approaches. Men in Kosovo are already exposed to physical and psychological violence during adolescence; they witness their mothers and sisters being marginalized and then normalize and socialize such behavior toward their peers and later toward their partners. When sexual and gender-based violence occurs, politico-legal institutions tend to relativize these crimes and reconcile victims with their abusers, not respecting applicable law, thus perpetrating structural violence and harming the human security of the survivors. When artificial reconciliation is coerced, survivors are further exposed to violence. Since there are indications that previous exposure to sexual and gender-based violence, a track record of criminal offenses by the perpetrator, and the threatening of females with (or simply possession of) a weapon may culminate in femicide, institutions should be held responsible when they turn a blind eye to these warning signs. The mutually interdependent relationship between agents and the structure continuously reinforces victimizing approaches both among those agents and the structure itself. However, a slow change in these approaches is inevitable in constructivist theory. The question remains, how such a change can be catalyzed by raising the consciousness of both agents and the structure about sexual and gender-based related issues, since only agents and the structure can do so.

DISCLOSURE STATEMENT

The author reports there are no competing interests to declare.

FUNDING

This publication was written at Masaryk University with support from a Specific University Research Grant provided by the Ministry of Education, Youth, and Sports of the Czech Republic.

ORCID

Jiří Němec http://orcid.org/0000-0003-1028-1275

RECOMMENDED READINGS

Agency for Gender Equality of Kosovo. 2020. "Raporti nga Policia e Kosoves për Vitin 2019" (Report of the Kosovo Police for the Year 2019). *Office of the Prime Minister of*

Kosovo: Agency for Gender Equality of Kosovo, March 11, 2020. https://abgj.rks-gov.net/al/publikimet/106/raporte-dhe-hulumtime.

Amnesty International. 2017. "'Wounds That Burn Our Souls': Compensation for Kosovo's Wartime Rape Survivors, But Still No Justice." *Amnesty International*, December 13, 2017. https://www.amnesty.org/en/wp-content/uploads/2021/05/EUR7075582017ENGLISH.pdf

Assembly of the Republic of Kosovo. 2014. "Ligji Nr. 04/L-172 për Ndryshimin dhe Plotëdimin e Ligjit Nr. 04/L-154 për Statusin dhe të Drejtat e Dëshmorëve, Invalidëve, Veteranëve, Pjesëtarëve të Ushtrisë Çlirimtare të Kosovës, Viktimave të Dhunës Sexuale të Luftës, Viktimave Civile dhe Familjarëve të Tyre" (Law No. 04/L-172 on Amending and Supplementing the Law No. 04/L-154 on the Status and the Rights of the Martyrs, Invalids, Veterans, Members of Kosovo Liberation Army, Sexual Violence Victims of the War, Civilian Victims and their Families). http://old.kuvendikosoves.org/common/docs/ligjet/04-L-172%20sh.pdf

Bami, Xhorxhina. 2021. "No More! Kosovars Hold Vigils for Latest Femicide Victim." *Balkan Investigative Reporting Network: Prishtina Insight*, March 19, 2021. https://prishtinainsight.com/no-more-kosovars-hold-vigils-for-latest-femicide-victim/

Bami, Xhorxhina. 2022. "Kosovo Activists Request Maximum Sentencing in Latest Femicide." *Balkan Investigative Reporting Network: Prishtina Insight*, January 6, 2022. https://prishtinainsight.com/kosovo-activists-request-maximum-sentencing-in-latest-femicide/

Banjska, Endrita, Besarta Breznica, David J. J. Ryan, and Nicole Fransworth. 2021. "From Laws to Action: Monitoring the Institutional Response to Gender-based Violence in Kosovo," Lauren Hanna (ed.). *Kosovo Women's Network*. https://womensnetwork.org/wp-content/uploads/2021/05/KWN-GBV-Report-ENG-Final-2.pdf

Campbell, Jacquelyn C., Daniel Webster, Jane Koziol-McLain, Carolyn Block, Doris Campbell, Mary Ann Curry, Faye Gary, et al. 2003. "Risk Factors for Femicide in Abusive Relationships: Results from a Multisite Case Control Study." *American Journal of Public Health* 93 (7): 1089–1097. doi:10.2105/ajph.93.7.1089.

Carey, David, Jr, and M. Gabriela Torres. 2020. "Precursors to Femicide: Guatemalan Women in a Vortex of Violence." *The Latin American Research Review* 45 (3): 142–164.

Dekel, Bianca, and Michelle Andipatin. 2016. "Abused Women's Understanding of Intimate Partner Violence and the Link to Intimate Femicide." *Forum Qualitative Sozialforschung* 17 (1): 1–30. doi:10.17169/fqs-17.1.2394.

EULEX. 2020. "Justice Monitoring Report: Findings and Recommendations: September 2019 – Mid-March 2020." *European Union Rule of Law Mission in Kosovo*. https://www.eulex-kosovo.eu/eul/repository/docs/19102020_EU%20Rule%20of%20Law%20Mission%20Justice%20_EN.pdf

Hernández, Wilson. 2021. "Violence with Femicide Risk: Its Effects on Women and Their Children." *Journal of Interpersonal Violence* 36 (11-12): NP6465–NP6491. November 28, 2018. doi:10.1177/0886260518815133.

Justice Rapid Response. 2019. "Guest Article: Kosovo Leads the Way in Reparations for Victims of Conflict-Related Sexual Violence". *Justice Rapid Response*, December 9, 2019. https://www.justicerapidresponse.org/guest-article-kosovo-leads-the-way-in-reparations-for-victims-of-conflict-related-sexual-violence/

Kerr, Pauline. 2007. "Human Security," in Alan Collins (ed.), *Contemporary Security Studies*, 91–108. Oxford: Oxford University Press.

Kosovo Women's Network. 2020. "KWN Condemns the Reduction of the Sentence for Pjetër Ndrecaj." *Kosovo Women's Network*, September 14, 2020. https://womensnetwork.org/kwn-condemns-the-reduction-of-the-sentence-for-pjeter-ndrecaj/

Limanu, Laura, and Hana Marku. 2014. "The Problem with the Kosovo War Rape Petition." *Balkan Investigative Reporting Network: Balkan Insight: Balkan Transitional Justice*, July 23, 2014. https://balkaninsight.com/2014/07/23/the-problem-with-the-kosovowar-rape-petition/

OSAC. 2020. "Kosovo 2020 Crime and Safety Report." *United States Department of State: Bureau of Diplomatic Security: Overseas Security Advisory Council*, December 29, 2021. https://www.osac.gov/Content/Report/fde86eb1-52a0-47aabc44-190e3de705a5

OSCE Mission in Kosovo and UNFPA Kosovo. 2018. "A Men's Perspective on Gender Equality in Kosovo: Main findings from the International Men and Gender Equality Survey (IMAGES). *Organization for Security and Co-operation in Europe and United Nations Population Fund.* https://www.osce.org/files/f/documents/7/e/382507.pdf

OSCE. 1999. "Kosovo/Kosova: As seen, as told." *The Organization for Security and Cooperation in Europe: The Office for Democratic Institutions and Human Rights.* https://www.osce.org/files/f/documents/d/d/17772.pdf

Subotic', Gordana, and Adriana Zaharijevic'. 2018. "Women between War Scylla and Nationalist Charybdis: Legal Interpretations of Sexual Violence in Countries of Former Yugoslavia," in John I. Lahai and Moyo Khanyisela (eds.), *Gender in Human Rights and Transitional Justice*. Cham: Palgrave Macmillan. Advance online publication. doi: 10.1007/978-3-319-54202-7_9.

UNGA. 2005. "General Assembly Resolution 60/147: Basic Principles and Guidelines on the Right to a Remedy and Reparation for Victims of Gross Violations of International Human Rights Law and Serious Violations of International Humanitarian Law, A/RES/60/147." *United Nations*, March 21, 2006. https://undocs.org/en/A/RES/60/147

United Nations. 2020. "The Handbook for United Nations Field Missions on Preventing and Responding to Conflict-Related Sexual Violence." *The United Nations.* https://peacemaker.un.org/sites/peacemaker.un.org/files/United%20Nations_CRSV%20Handbook.pdf

WHO. 2012. "Understanding and Addressing Violence Against Women: Femicide." *World Health Organization*, 1–8. https://apps.who.int/iris/bitstream/handle/10665/77421/WHO_RHR_12.38_eng.pdf?s

WHO. 2021. "Violence Against Women: Factors Associated with Intimate Partner Violence and Sexual Violence Against Women." *World Health Organization*, March 9, 2021. https://www.who.int/news-room/fact-sheets/detail/violence-against-women

The Continuum of Human Insecurity for Women: Femicide in War and Peace

LAURA ISABELLA BRUNKE AND TOBIAS DEBIEL

Many post-conflict countries are characterized by a lack of human security. Women are particularly affected by violent crimes, sometimes akin to or even more than during armed conflict. Only recently has attention been drawn to femicides. Why does femicide appear to transcend between war and peace? How can the (human) security of women be improved in the long-term through a profound process of societal conflict transformation? This article answers these questions with an empirical focus on how the past of internal armed conflict was dealt with in Latin America. The region experienced state terrorism by military dictatorships in the second half of the 20th century and is one of the most insecure places for women today. Our concrete research aims are threefold: First, to locate femicide on a continuum of human insecurity between war and peace; second, to make gender-related killings committed during dictatorship visible as femicides, not solely sexualized crimes; and third, to highlight the need for a more comprehensive gender-critical human security concept. The article interprets achievements in international criminal justice as well as the increasing social protest against gendered crimes in Latin America as a starting point for a "Conflict Transformation 2.0."

INTRODUCTION

Violence against women (VAW) is a pervasive element of war. It is also a pervasive element of societies which are formally at peace, as well as of every other transitional phase in between. Yet, there is often an overlooked link between different phases. More than three decades ago, British Sociologist Kelly (1987) conceptualized women's experiences of sexual and gender-based violence (SGBV) on a continuum, exposing the relationships between multiple types of violence and questioning the separation between the private and the public. Complemented by a spatial and temporal dimension, the term 'continuum' is equally useful to show how VAW transcends between war and peace and vice versa in specific geopolitical locations (Cockburn 2004). This research is dedicated to the relationship between femicide (gender-related killings of women and girls) in violent conflict and its aftermath, so-called post-conflict societies. Our analytical focus is on states which have experienced asymmetric intra-state warfare in the form of dictatorships.

In the aftermath of armed conflict, the primary political objective is to weaken the probability of a relapse into violence, and in doing so, increase the probability of a sustainable peace. The question is, peace for whom? Since the mid-1990s, the concept of human security has promoted a people-centered approach to post-conflict peacebuilding. In this sense, the human security paradigm challenges the formerly hegemonic state security focus and emphasizes complex human needs in parallel to national security concerns. However, as Reardon (2018, 15) critically observes, "the conditions [for human security] are seldom, if ever, fully met, even in times of so-called peace." In particular, personal integrity rights of women and other vulnerable groups, such as gender and sexual minorities, remain compromised. Oftentimes, the violence lives on, sometimes even in similar prevalence and forms as during armed conflict.

Our target phenomenon, femicide, belongs to the personal security dimension of this (still evolving) security concept. Considering that femicide is a critical security issue in both war and peace, it is a prime example for how violence can transcend between these phases. Can this problem be explained by the way states deal with a past of internal armed conflict? How can the (human) security of women be improved in the long-term through a profound process of societal conflict transformation? We discuss these questions with special reference to Latin America which experienced state terrorism by military dictatorships in the second half of the 20th century and is one of the most insecure places for women today. Our concrete research aims are threefold: First, to locate femicide on a continuum of human insecurity between war and peace; second, to make gender-related killings committed during dictatorship visible as femicides, not solely sexualized crimes; and third, to highlight the need for a more comprehensive gender-critical human security concept.

HUMAN INSECURITY AFTER WAR AND DICTATORSHIP

Men and women experience armed conflict and its aftermath differently. For women, post-conflict situations are often not only associated with relief but can be disproportionately overshadowed by memories of gender-based suffering in addition to other forms also experienced by men (Cockburn 2004, 35-36). Although collectively organized violence normally significantly decreases after war or dictatorship, VAW does not necessarily; instead, it can remain at a high level or even increase (Pankhurst 2007; Hristov 2020). In many cases, home forms only a perceived safe space as the violence perpetrated by intimate partners and relatives is perpetuated. In the public sphere, the incomplete consolidation of the rule of law adds another insecurity factor. Women's physical insecurity in the private and public sphere is accompanied by socioeconomic disruption and precarious livelihoods (Berry 2017, 831), as well as a risk of a patriarchal 'backlash' in response to new political gains (Walby 1993, 76). Various conditions interact, among others "war trauma, an increased availability of weapons, heightened alcoholism and drug use, and the celebration of militarized masculinity during periods of armed conflict" (Berry 2017, 844).

The manifold threats to women's lives cannot be captured by classical concepts of security which establish the state as the referent object. It is therefore useful to recall human security as a conceptual framework, as first presented by the United Nations Development Programme (UNDP) in 1994 in the Human Development Report. It elevated the individual to the primary referent object of security considerations. This was innovative in two respects: First, it made clear that the individual can also be significantly threatened by states and their repressive apparatuses in the dimensions of personal and political security. In this way, it highlighted the Janus-faced character of the state as both guarantor and endangerer of the physical and psychological integrity of the individual. Second, UNDP focused on particularly vulnerable groups in the field of personal security, thus identifying at an early stage an area that the UN Security Council (UNSC) would later take up in numerous resolutions on the protection of civilians and the role of women in conflict. The concept of human security, at the same time, goes beyond the understanding of the UNSC insofar as the latter focuses on the issue of sexualized violence with a view to its threats to world peace and less on the vulnerable individual (Hitzel-Cassagnes and Martinsen 2021, 93, 101).

The Commission on Human Security (CHR 2003) developed the UNDP concept further and, following Alkire (2003, 2), focused on protecting a "vital core" of every human being from serious, far-reaching threats. In addition to the protection of fundamental rights and freedoms, this also implies enabling a life in dignity. However, as meritorious as the still crucial concepts by UNDP and the CHR are, they also need to be criticized and further developed from a feminist perspective. For one, the report Human Security Now (CHR 2003) failed to independently conceptualize the importance of human security for women. Instead, women were described primarily as beings in need of protection, and tellingly mentioned in the same breath as children (Tripp 2013, 12). Moreover, the UNDP and CHR concepts are very much in the liberal tradition of the Enlightenment. Accordingly, they assume that individuals are first and foremost autonomous and rationally acting subjects in the Kantian sense. This, however, does not sufficiently consider social hierarchies, dependencies, and power relations (Marhia 2013, 19, 26) as they exist especially in patriarchally structured gender relations. Against this background, we argue with Tripp (2013, 6) for taking up the concept of human security in its positive and emancipatory elements but expanding it to include a "a more proactive notion of peace that requires addressing the structural issues that give rise to violence." To illustrate this point, we choose the human rights violation femicide as a global security concern.

FEMICIDE AS A (CONTESTED) GLOBAL SECURITY CONCERN

"The world can never be at peace unless people have security in their daily lives."
(UNDP Human Development Report 1994, 1)

Femicide is the intentional murder of women (and girls) for gender-related reasons. As such, it is the epitome of gendered violence and a central security concern for women. Within UNDP's human security paradigm, femicide classifies under the *personal security* dimension which is defined as "protecting people from physical violence, whether from the state or external states, from violent individuals or sub-state factors, from domestic abuse and from predatory adults" (Acharya 2011, 480). A woman's personal security is, evidently, annulled by death. However, under the human security concept, the fear of becoming a victim of femicide must also be considered as a psychological burden for individual women and, in some cases, entire societies.

Men and women die different deaths. Whereas men are more likely to be intentionally killed overall, their deaths are mostly related to organized or ordinary crime, not gender. Hence, they are mainly, though not exclusively, associated with traditional human security concerns related to the rule of law. Also, men are overwhelmingly killed by other men. Women, on the other hand, are disproportionately murdered within their immediate social circles, namely by intimate partners, or other family members (see so-called honor-based or dowry-related crimes). In 2017, the United Nations Office on Drugs and Crime (UNODC 2019, 10) documented 87,000 intentional murders of women, most of which were committed by men, for gender-related reasons (58 percent). This translates to almost 6 out of 10 murdered women and only includes those femicides which occurred in the private sphere. In addition, there are gender-related killings committed by strangers in the public sphere, for example, related to sexual objectification and economic exploitation.

Most of the countries analyzed in the UNODC Global Homicide Report are those currently not involved in violent conflict or war. So, is this peace then? Many feminist scholars disagree. They describe the omnipresence of lethal violence in women's everyday lives as a "low-intensity warfare waged on women's bodies" (Fregoso and Bejarano 2010, 1), a "battlefield" (Monárrez 2012, 197) or even a variant of "genocide" (Scheper-Hughes 2003; Lagarde 2004; Banerji 2009; Waites 2018; Standish 2021). The conceptual appropriateness of the genocide analogy (which would have implicit consequences under international law) has been critically discussed (Weil 2016; Standish 2021). Yet, there exists an overarching consensus that the violent situation of women, indeed, resembles armed conflict; not only in prevalence, but also in forms (Sigsworth and Valji 2012, 115). Men asphyxiate, strangulate, beat, stab, shoot, set on fire or mutilate women, causing some of the most painful forms of death (UNODC 2019, 22). It is not uncommon to hear about cases where women were stabbed dozens of times by their intimate partners. Moreover, non-intimate murders are often preceded by sexual violence and torture. Many victims are raped before they are killed.

An asymmetric power relationship between men and women, not only in terms of physical force but also social hierarchy, underscores these crimes. Men murder women to reinforce their control over them (Corradi et al. 2016, 5). In the personal sphere, femicide victims are oftentimes those women who 'disrespected' men (or societal expectations of women). In the context of non-intimate femicides, female bodies are treated as disposable commodities (e.g., organized or ordinary crime). In conflict zones, women are targeted to humiliate and weaken the (male) enemy, turning femicide, alongside rape, sexual slavery, forced sterilization and sexual torture, into a tool, or even strategy, of war (Manjoo and McRaith 2011). Critical feminism identifies patriarchy as the unifying component underlying different 'private' and 'public' sources of gender inequality (Walby 1990). Patriarchal systems distribute more (or sometimes even exclusive) economic, social, and political capital to males, while also legitimizing VAW and impunity for these types of crimes. Being murdered because of one's gender makes femicide the indisputably most serious manifestation of gender inequality. Nonetheless, femicide is seldom on (human) security agendas, in war or peace.

THE WAR/PEACE NEXUS OF FEMICIDE: EXPERIENCES FROM LATIN AMERICA

Human insecurity for women is often a problem of invisible continuities (Cockburn 2004). What concerns Latin America, the present can be elucidated by turning to the region's past of internal armed conflict during the era of the Cold War. These violent experiences, so we argue, drive today's high femicide rates through the perpetuation of militarized concepts of gender and sexuality. To begin, we must turn to the mid- to late 20th century when right-wing military dictatorships came to power by method of coup d'état in most states in the region. The primary target of the military, as well as that of paramilitaries, death squads and militias which operated under their mandate, were guerilla groups, which actively (and violently) propagated socialist ideas. However, ordinary citizens from the left political spectrum assumed to be sympathizers with the socialist cause were equally persecuted and violently abducted, tortured or otherwise abused and disappeared. The state terror committed in this epoch against 'internal enemies' amounted to the worst crimes known in international law: genocide, crimes against humanity and war crimes.

What is less discussed, is the element of VAW which underpinned state terror. Research shows that Marxist rebel groups were less likely to use violence against civilians, including gender-based forms (Balcells and Kalyvas 2010), pointing toward crucial ideological differences between conflict actors. The field of military sociology, dedicated to the systematic study of military institutions, has provided important insights by exposing a gendered dimension underlying the crimes committed by Latin American dictatorships. First and foremost, these were led by patriarchal ideas of power and violence and sought to reinforce rigid gender roles and hierarchies. Women belonged in the private sphere of the home. Their political participation in the public sphere, which was reserved for men, contradicted prevailing conservative norms – as did any other form of political or sexual liberation, such as extra- and premarital sex or homosexuality (Manzano 2014, 2). In their role as self-proclaimed 'guardians of the family institution' and Christian values, the military declared 'guerilla women' as a threat to the nation (ibid, 27). Across the region, most captured women were victims of some form of sexual violence in addition to other forms of torture also experienced by men. Moreover, women were sometimes specifically targeted to humiliate or punish male guerilas or sympathizers. Their bodies symbolized the honor of the enemy (Hristov 2020, 42). Violence was either instrumentalized and ordered by superiors (see, for example, Guatemala or Colombia) or opportunistic, taking advantage of prisoners who were physically and psychologically exhausted and isolated (Joffily 2016, 172). Thousands of women were later brutally assassinated like their male counterparts. Others survived to share their gendered experiences.

When the world's first truth commissions and trials were founded in Latin America to address human rights violations during authoritarian rule, the public/private divide was still thriving as a concept. As Sigsworth and Valji (2012, 120) explain, "Until relatively recently, international [and domestic] law related to conflict and post-conflict issues was distinctly ungendered in that it paid no attention to women's different positioning to men during and in the aftermath of conflict. Instead, it adopted as its starting point men's experiences of conflict in the public sphere." Reports by truth commissions, such as those from Argentina, Chile, Brazil, and Uruguay, confirm this observation. Women were successfully incorporated into transitional justice processes when they had experienced similar types of violence as men. Disappearances, assassinations, and torture were considered worthy of investigation and sometimes prosecution. However, incidents of VAW are only documented in the form of anecdotes or general observations (Joffily 2016, 196), thus, denying the full extent of the practice. This undifferentiated procedure not only trivialized women's gendered experiences, but also meant that "a patriarchal gender order [was] once again established" in the new post-conflict era (Berry 2017, 832). Dictatorships left a legacy of normalized violence (against women) and "cultures of masculinity prone to violence" (Cockburn 2004, 44).

Today, many of these murders of women committed during armed conflict would (and should) be considered femicides, both conceptually and legally. Yet, in the absence of social, political, and legal reforms, which explicitly acknowledge past gendered inequalities, they are not. Against the background of an undealt with past, Latin America has constructed a continuum of human insecurity. The violence "may have differing motivations in different contexts, [however, the] net effect is the same" (Sigsworth and Valji 2012, 115): The region remains one of the most lethal for women (UNODC 2019, 18). The war/peace binary is, therefore, false and we must wonder, (how) can conflict transformation still be achieved?

CONFLICT TRANSFORMATION 2.0: TOWARD TRANSFORMATIVE JUSTICE?

Post-conflict societies, such as those which have recovered from state terrorism, increasingly utilize transitional justice mechanisms and measures to 'deal with the past.' For women, transitional justice is still ambivalent. Periods of transition can encompass opportunity structures for a redefinition of gender norms or greater political participation (Berry 2017, 831). In nascent democracies, for example, new laws and institutions are commonly established to this end. Yet, it is not enough to create norms and institutions, insofar as there is often an implementation gap and discriminated and marginalized groups have more difficult access to the justice system. Nonetheless, the legal dimension represents an important linchpin, where conflict transformation in the context of crimes against women should begin and gross human insecurity can be overcome. In other words, "justice reform must include an agenda to prioritize SGBV crimes and women's access to justice, in order to mitigate against impunity and the continued rise in crimes of SGBV" (Sigsworth and Valiji 2012, 127–128).

International criminal justice has set precedence for national legal systems. As early as 1998, the International Criminal Tribunal for Rwanda (ICTR) made a landmark decision with the conviction of Jean-Paul Akayesu when it established for the first time in international jurisprudence that rape is part of genocide and crimes against humanity (Björkdahl and Selimovic 2021, 76–77). The Rome Statute to the International Criminal Court (ICC) in the same year defined SGBV in the context of violent crimes and considered "not only rape but also sexual slavery, enforced pregnancy, enforced sterilization and enforced prostitution" (ibid, 78). Overcoming impunity for certain crimes against women, particularly rape and sexual violence, was also called for in the UN Women, Peace and Security Agenda and respective UNSC resolutions, starting with Resolution 1325 in 2000, which linked the issue to international peace. However, a central concern is that transitional justice, whether at the international or national level, is usually accompanied by a hierarchization of human rights crimes, meaning that the criminal justice system focuses on specific offenses only (Buckley-Zistel and Zolkos 2012, 10). This leads to some individuals being recognized as victims of dictatorship and war, while others remain invisible (O'Rourke 2012, 147–148), contradicting the idea of 'indivisible' human rights. For a long time, gender-based crimes were completely absent from the agenda. Now, Swaine (2018, 271) criticizes, "a focus on sexualized violence pushes open space to see sexualized harms, yet closes down the space to address variant violences in conflict." Indeed, whereas rape and other sexual crimes against women have become salient in public discourse on conflict and war, killings of women and girls continue to be lumped together with those of men regardless of gender-specific dimensions. Many femicides become 'nothing more' than homicide. In consequence, VAW is made invisible and militarized masculinities with high conflict potential transition into the post-conflict era (Hudson 2021, 145–146). On this basis, we argue for femicide to be integrated in post-conflict human security discourse, thereby making the concept more gender-critical.

Concretely translated, a feminist understanding of human security means that transitional justice, which has so far been oriented more toward formal institutions, is further developed into a transformative justice that focuses not only on the state but also on local communities and their everyday lives (Gready and Robins 2014, 340). Transformative justice is not primarily top-down but shaped by bottom-up processes. In Latin America, there is evidence for hope if we turn to delayed forms of gendered justice. What concerns women's insecurity during periods of peace, a new wave of feminist movements has gained momentum across the region and secured significant progress through the visibility of femicide and subsequent codification in domestic legal systems. In parallel, civil society activism has encouraged progress on gendered justice for sexual crimes committed under dictatorships (see recent landmark judgments in Guatemala, Chile, and Argentina). If feminist demands in peace and war were to be united, and expanded beyond the narrow framing of SGBV, these causes hold the potential to promote a holistic understanding of femicide along a continuum of human insecurity, thereby revealing largely invisible interlinkages.

CONCLUSION

Post-conflict societies are at the crossroads. The absence of armed conflicts or repressive dictatorships often does not translate into positive peace. This is especially true for women, who continue to be subjected to violence in both private and public spaces—up to its most extreme form, femicide. The concept of human security has the potential to highlight these invisible crimes if it overcomes its blind spots regarding gender-specific insecurities and takes into account the social embedding of people in patriarchal structures. Transitional justice will also have to change in the sense of transformative justice. Most importantly, this means a differentiated view of the experiences that men and women have with violence in war, dictatorship, and post-conflict situations. All too often, women's experiences of violence are only addressed when they resemble those of men. Moreover, the entire continuum of violence, including cultural and discursive manifestations, must be considered. This requires "disarming the hegemonic form of [militarized] masculinity that privileges and sustains violence in the conduct of social relations," thereby creating 'citizen-soldiers' in post-conflict societies (O'Rourke 2012, 157).

Fortunately, when it comes to protection from violence, progress does not solely depend on the state and its institutions. The UNSC has spoken out, albeit inconsistently, in favor of ending impunity for crimes of sexualized violence. Not least, the ICC has recognized forms of VAW as genocide, war crimes and crimes against humanity. At last, in Latin America—a region whose experience we have used to illustrate how femicide transcends between war and peace—social protests have led to the typification of the crime in domestic legislation and legal precedents in relation to past gendered harms of a sexualized nature. Considering this momentum, transformative justice is on the horizon. Both, soldiers and citizen-soldiers are increasingly facing a 'backlash' of their own.

RECOMMENDED READINGS

Acharya, Amitav. 2011. "Human Security," in John Baylis, Steve Smith and Patricia Owens (eds.), *The Globalization of World Politics: An Introduction to International Relations*, 487–493. Oxford: Oxford University Press.

Alkire, Sabina. 2003. "A Conceptual Framework for Human Security." Crise Working Paper No. 2/2003 (Centre for Research on Inequality, Human Security and Ethnicity, CRISE, University of Oxford), Oxford.

Balcells, Laia, and Stathis Kalyvas. 2010. "Did Marxism make a difference? Marxist rebellions and national liberation movements." September 2010. Accessed 10 January 2022. https://citeseerx.ist.psu.edu/viewdoc/download?doi=10.1.1.985.5246&rep=rep1&type=pdf

Banerji, Rita. 2009. *Sex and Power: Defining History, Shaping Societies*. London: Penguin Global.

Berry, Marie. 2017. "Barriers to Women's Progress after Atrocities: Evidence from Rwanda and Bosnia-Herzegovina." *Gender & Society* 31 (6):830–853. doi: 10.1177/0891243217737060.

Björkdahl, Annika, and Johanna Selimovic. 2021. "Gender and Transnational Justice," in Olivera Simić (ed.), *An Introduction to Transnational Justice*, 73–95. London/New York: Routledge.

Buckley-Zistel, Susanne, and Magdalena Zolkos. 2012. "Introduction: Gender in Transitional Justice," in Susanne Buckley-Zistel and Ruth Stanley (eds.), *Gender in Transitional Justice*, 1–33. Basingstoke: Palgrave Macmillan.

CHR (Commission on Human Security). 2003. *Human Security Now*. New York: United Nations.

Cockburn, Cynthia. 2004. "The Continuum of Violence: A Gender Perspective on War and Peace," in Wenona Giles and Jennifer Hyndman (eds.), *Sites of Violence: Gender and Conflict Zones*, 24–44. California: University of California Press.

Corradi, Consuelo, Chaime Marcuello-Servos, Santiago Boira, and Shalva Weil. 2016. "Theories of Femicide and Their Significance for Social Research." *Current Sociology* 64 (7):975–995. doi:10.1177/0011392115622256.

Fregoso, Rosa-Linda, and Cynthia Bejarano. 2010. "Introduction. A Cartography of Feminicide in the Americas," in Rosa-Linda Fregoso and Cynthia Bejarano (eds.), *Terrorizing Women. Feminicide in the Americas*, 1–42. Durham: Duke University Press.

Gready, Paul, and Simon Robins. 2014. "From Transitional to Transformative Justice: A New Agenda for Practice." *International Journal of Transitional Justice* 8 (3):339–361. doi:10.1093/ijtj/iju013.

Hitzel-Cassagnes, Tanja, and Franziska Martinsen. 2021. "Sicherheit Und Sexualisierte Gewalt in (Post)konflikt- Gesellschaften: Zur Rolle Des Rechts Aus Feministischer Perspektive," in Antje Daniel, Rirhandu Mageza-Barthel and Melanie Richter-Montpetit (eds.), *Gewalt, Krieg Und Flucht. Feministische Pespektiven Auf Sicherheit*, 97–117. Opladen: Verlag Barbara Budrich.

Hristov, Jasmin. 2020. "Armed Actors, the Commodification of Women, and the Destruction of Childhood: Understanding the Connections between Predatory Sexuality and the Violence of Capital in Colombia," in Samuel Cohn and Rae Lesser Blumberg (eds.), *Gender and Development: The Economic Basis of Women's Power*, 31–64. California: SAGE.

Hudson, Heidi. 2021. "It Matters How You 'Do' Gender in Peacebuilding: African Approaches and Challenges." *Insight on Africa* 13 (2):142–159. doi:10.1177/0975087820987154.

Joffily, Mariana. 2016. "Sexual Violence in the Military Dictatorships of Latin America: Who Wants to Know?" *Sur* 13 (24):165–176.

Kelly, Liz. 1987. "The Continuum of Sexual Violence," in Jalna Hanmer and Mary Maynard (eds.), *Women, Violence and Social Control. Explorations in Sociology*, (British Sociological Association Conference Volume series), 46–60. London: Palgrave Macmillan.

Lagarde, Marcela. 2004. "Por la vida y la libertad de las mujeres. Fin al feminicidio." February 2004. Accessed 7 January 2022. http://archivos.diputados.gob.mx/Comisiones/Especiales/Feminicidios/docts/mlagardefeminicidio.pdf

Manjoo, Rashina, and Calleigh McRaith. 2011. "Gender-Based Violence and Justice in Conflict and Post-Conflict Areas." *Cornell International Law Journal* 44 (11):11–31.

Manzano, Valeria. 2014. "Sex, Gender and the Making of the 'Enemy within' in Cold War Argentina." *Journal of Latin American Studies* 47 (1):1–29. doi:10.1017/S0022216X14000686.

Marhia, Natasha. 2013. "Some Humans Are More Human than Others: Troubling the 'Human' in Human Security from a Critical Feminist Perspective." *Security Dialogue* 44 (1):19–35. doi:10.1177/0967010612470293.

Monárrez, Julia. 2012. "Violencia Extrema y Existencia Precaria en Ciudad Juárez." *Frontera Norte* 24:191–199.

O'Rourke, Catherine. 2012. "Transitioning to What? Transitional Justice and Gendered Citizenship in Chile and Colombia," in Susanne Buckley-Zistel and Ruth Stanley (eds.), *Gender in Transitional Justice*, 136–160. Basingstoke: Palgrave Macmillan.

Reardon, Betty. 2018. "Women and Human Security: A Feminist Framework and Critique of the Prevailing Patriarchal Security System," in Betty Reardon and Asha Hans (eds.), *The Gender Imperative: Human Security vs. State Security*, 7–36. India: Routledge.

Scheper-Hughes, Nancy. 2003. "The Genocidal Continuum: Peace-Time Crimes," in Jeanette Mageo (ed.), *Power and the Self*, 29–47. Cambridge: Cambridge University Press.

Sigsworth, Romi, and Nahla Valji. 2012. "Continuities of Violence against Women and the Limitations of Transitional Justice: The Case of South Africa," in Susanne Buckley-Zistel and Ruth Stanley (eds.), *Gender in Transitional Justice*, 115–135. Basingstoke: Palgrave Macmillan.

Standish, Katerina. 2021. "Everyday Genocide: Femicide, Transicide and the Responsibility to Protect." *Journal of Aggression, Conflict and Peace Research*. ahead-of-print. doi:10.1108/JACPR-10-2021-0642.

Swaine, Aisling. 2018. *Conflict-Related Violence against Women: Transforming Transition*. Cambridge: Cambridge University Press.

Tripp, Aili Mari. 2013. "Toward a Gender Perspective on Human Security," in Aili Mari Tripp, Maira Ferree and Christina Ewig (eds.), *Gender, Violence, and Human Security: Critical Feminist Perspectives*, 1–32. New York, USA: New York University Press.

UNDP (United Nations Development Programme). 1994. *Human Development Report*. Oxford: Oxford University Press.

UNODC (United Nations Office on Drugs and Crime). 2019. *Global Study on Homicide*. Vienna.

Waites, Matthew. 2018. "Genocide and Global Queer Politics." *Journal of Genocide Research* 20 (1):44–67. doi:10.1080/14623528.2017.1358920.

Walby, Sylvia. 1990. *Theorizing Patriarchy*. Oxford: Blackwell.

Walby, Sylvia. 1993. "Backlash' in Historical Context," in Mary Kennedy, Cathy Lubelska, and Val Walsh (eds.), *Making Connections: Women's Studies. Women's Movements, Women's Lives*, 79–89. London: Taylor & Francis.

Weil, Shalva. 2016. "Making Femicide Visible." *Current Sociology* 64 (7):1124–1137. doi:10.1177/0011392115623602.

Statistical Biases, Measurement Challenges, and Recommendations for Studying Patterns of Femicide in Conflict

MARIA GARGIULO

Collecting data on conflict mortality—including data on femicide—is difficult and can be dangerous. The resulting data is often incomplete and not statistically representative of the victim population as a whole. Data on femicide in conflict suffers from additional complications due to measurement challenges stemming from definitional and operational ambiguities. Despite these difficulties, as more and higher quality data on femicide becomes available, there are new opportunities to use statistical methods to study patterns of violence, which can help inform policy and accountability efforts. However, this data needs to be used carefully: drawing population level inferences from incomplete datasets risks misunderstanding the true underlying dynamics of the violence. This article explores the challenges and opportunities of collecting and analyzing data on femicide and offers four recommendations for data collectors and data analysts.

INTRODUCTION

The Guatemalan *Comisión para el Esclarecimiento Histórico* (CEH) documented 1,465 cases of sexual violence during the internal armed conflict from 1960–1996. In 25% of these cases, the victims—who were primarily Mayan women and girls—were subsequently executed (CEH. 1999). Based on the available contextual information, most, if not all, of these killings could be classified as femicides.[1] These killings, however, likely only represent a partial accounting of all of the femicides that

---
[1] Femicide (or feminicide) refers to the misogynistic killing of women and girls by men. The term femicide was formalized by Radford and Russell (1992). Building on this work, Lagarde y de los Ríos (2010) introduced the term feminicide in English (*feminicidio* in Spanish), which is commonly used in Latin America, to situate these killings as violations of women's human rights and to highlight the role that the state plays in allowing this violence through impunity.

occurred during the conflict due to missing data. Deducing statistical patterns of femicide using these data alone is likely to misstate the true underlying patterns of femicidal violence. In the case of femicide, missingness generally takes two forms: (1) instances where victims' deaths are documented, but lack contextual information that allows them to be classified as femicides; and (2) instances where a death goes undocumented altogether. The result often understates the magnitude of the violence that occurred, and has the potential to distort our understanding of patterns of violence.

This problem is not unique to femicide—it is a well-documented challenge that affects data collected in conflict settings[2]—although femicide poses additional challenges to documentation efforts. Additionally, the difficulty of missing data also affects femicide documentation in times of peace. Even in places where femicide or feminicide is explicitly criminalized, governments have largely failed to publish official statistics that are reliable, complete, and regularly updated. Furthermore, reporting femicide through official channels (e.g., through the police) is stigmatized and dangerous in many contexts, and cultures of impunity often prevent proper investigations when femicides are reported. Activists, journalists, and civil society groups have begun assembling their own datasets of femicide victims to fill the voids left by official statistics.[3] These new datasets have surpassed the utility of official government data in many contexts,[4] but challenges with their use remain. Although these datasets are often more complete than the data made available by governments, they still suffer from missingness and are unlikely to be statistically representative of the entire population of victims. Drawing generalized conclusions from incomplete data risks misunderstanding the scale, scope, and patterns of violence. If quantitative methods are used to study femicide, the statistics that result must be correct. Anything less risks undermining our arguments and does a disservice to the victims, many of whose stories have not yet been told, and their families and loved ones.

---

[2]While this article focuses on conflict, challenges with missing data can also be present in situations of high levels of violence not necessarily classified as conflict.

[3]María Salguero's map of feminicide victims in Mexico (https://feminicidiosmx.crowdmap.com/), Helena Suárez Val's project "Feminicidio Uruguay" (Suárez Val 2021), and Rosalind Page's project "Black Femicide - U.S." (Vargas 2022) are some examples of activist data collection efforts. D'Ignazio and Klein (2020) provide further discussion of María Salguero's mapping efforts, using them as an example of how missing data on femicides results from power imbalances.

[4]In her work reporting on feminicide in Mexico, Alice Driver commented that "the most accurate records of feminicide are still kept by individuals, researchers, and journalists, rather than by the police or a state or federal institution" (Driver 2015, p. 15).

STATISTICAL BIASES IN CONFLICT DATA

Data that document conflict mortality—including data on femicides in conflict—are often incomplete; they tell true, but partial, narratives about the violence. Would-be witnesses might face stigmatization or retribution for reporting, violence might leave no surviving witnesses, or a body might never be identified. Data collection might be limited to urban areas that are easily accessible, organizational capacities might limit the amount of data that can be collected, and violence might threaten the safety of those collecting the data. The resulting samples are usually neither a complete census of the violence that occurred, nor a carefully constructed random sample. These non-exhaustive, non-probability samples are often referred to as "convenience samples," and they are commonly used to study armed conflict.[5] Some examples include testimonies presented to truth commissions or UN missions, service provision records from NGOs, and lists of victims compiled from media reports. The information provided by these sources is invaluable for conflict research, but an individual convenience sample is not appropriate for statistical inference on overarching patterns of violence because the data that are not recorded may be systematically different than the data that are recorded. This is the result of a statistical bias known as "selection bias," where victims are differentially selected into the sample because some victims are more legible to the data collectors than others. As a result, the data often reflect trends in documentation, rather than true trends in violence. This is not a critique of the data nor the data collection organizations, but rather a caution against "basing conclusions on inadequate analyses of raw data" (Price and Ball 2014).

Selection bias in conflict data can take many forms.[6] One example is event-size bias, the phenomenon by which large-fatality events generate more events than small-fatality reports. As a result, the likelihood of documenting a particular death depends on the size of the event in which the victim was killed.[7] Urban bias is another example. In this case, killings in urban areas are overrepresented because violence in rural areas could not be documented due to difficulties in physically accessing a location or

---

[5]For a more detailed overview about convenience samples and the complications of their use, see Price (2013).

[6]Dawkins (2021) provides an overview of several other types of biases that may affect reporting of conflict mortality data. While Dawkins focuses on the biases affecting newswire data in the context of conflict in South Sudan, the points raised are relevant to conflict data broadly.

[7]See Price and Ball (2014) and Carpenter, Fuller, and Roberts (2013) for further discussion, including empirical analyses of how event-size bias has impacted understanding of violence in conflicts in Syria and Iraq.

disruptions to cellular or internet connectivity, among other factors. A final example relates to social visibility: individuals who are well-networked within their communities and whose work is known at the national or international level, such as activists, are much more likely to have their killings documented than individuals who are not known at this scale.[8]

"Reporting bias" is another type of statistical bias that affects data documenting violence both in conflict and in peace. Reporting bias refers to the process by which cases are identified and subsequently documented, "[describing] how some [data] points become hidden, while others become visible" (Price and Ball 2014). Reporting bias is especially relevant to news media reports as it affects which victims are covered and how their stories are told. This is of particular importance to the study of femicide because news media reports form the basis of many of the lists of femicide victims currently kept by journalists, activists, and civil society groups. Media reporting on femicide tends to systematically exclude already marginalized populations and portrays certain deaths as "expected" or "acceptable," denying that these individuals should be considered victims. Examples of populations affected by these biases include indigenous women and girls (e.g., Grant et al. 2021), transgender and gender non-conforming individuals, sex workers, and individuals involved in drug trafficking (e.g., Velasco 2021). While lists of victims compiled from media sources provide valuable information, reporting biases underscore the need for caution when deducing statistical patterns from this data, particularly because reporting biases distort our understanding of violence perpetrated against highly vulnerable populations.

THE DIFFICULTY OF MEASURING FEMICIDE

Data that documents femicide is subject to additional challenges from definitional and operational ambiguities that complicate its use in quantitative analyses, both in conflict and peace. These ambiguities are less common when studying homicides generally, but there are parallels to other types of conflict-related killings. Civilian casualties are one such example, as different documentation groups may operationalize who counts as a

---

[8] Analyses on violence in the internal armed conflict in Colombia provide a useful avenue to study the impact of social visibility on documentation. For example, in studying the killings of social movement leaders between 2016–2018, Rozo Ángel and Ball (2019) estimate that there was little under-documentation of these killings after aggregating information from all available sources. In contrast, other studies of violence related to the conflict have demonstrated much higher levels of under-documentation (e.g., Guberek et al. 2010; Ball and Reed 2016).

civilian in different ways. For example, one group might rely on the clothing the victim was wearing at the time they were killed, another group might ask whether there were any military symbols nearby, and still another group might try to match the victim to a list of known combatants. These different operationalizations of civilian status can result in different understandings of patterns of violence.

Since the term was redefined by Diana Russell in 1976 at the International Tribunal on Crimes against Women, many different conceptualizations of femicide have emerged (Corradi et al. 2016). Similarly, incorporation of femicide into the legal sphere has not been uniform across the globe. For example, in Latin America, some countries have defined femicide or feminicide as an offense separate from homicide or manslaughter, whereas others instead added aggravating circumstances to existing crimes (ECLAC 2014). Even among the countries where femicide is criminalized as its own offense, the specific definition of the crime varies across the region, such that a killing that is considered a femicide in one country may not be considered as such in another country. There may also be variation in classification over time within the same jurisdiction. In the EU-27 countries and the UK, there is no uniform legal treatment of femicides in legal code, and femicides are instead classified as intentional homicides, non-intentional homicides, or manslaughter depending on national legal definitions (EIGE 2021). Related to data collection, femicide is also operationalized differently across documentation groups. As a result, even when documenting the same killings, different documentation groups can come to distinct conclusions depending on how femicide was operationalized (i.e., the criteria for classification) and the type of information that was collected.[9]

Nicaragua provides a useful case study to examine the impact of definitions on documentation because it is the only country in the world where the definition of femicide has been changed after being introduced into the penal code (Neumann 2022). The original definition passed in 2012 defined femicide as the murder of women by an intimate partner, family member, or stranger that happened in public or in private.[10] Two years later, a presidential executive order revised the definition to be limited to murders that occur in the context of an existing intimate relationship.[11] This definitional change subsequently altered the way that femicides were documented in government statistics. Perhaps

---

[9]See EIGE (2021) for a variety of comparisons between femicide measurement as conceptualized by governmental apparatuses, public femicide monitors, and NGOs. In particular, note that different organizations across Europe and internationally employ different definitions of femicide, collect different types of information, and have different criteria for classifying femicides.
[10]See *Ley Integral contra La Violencia hacia las Mujeres* (Law 779) Article IX.
[11]See Decreto 42-2014 in Nicaragua.

unsurprisingly, the government found that femicides declined after the definition was amended; in reality, many of the femicides that occurred in subsequent years were reallocated to other categories of lethal violence, ignoring the gendered dynamics of the killings (Neumann 2022). Femicides were not necessarily decreasing, but they certainly were more hidden in government reporting. Feminist organizations in Nicaragua have continued collecting data on femicides using the original definition and have observed large disparities between the numbers reported in government statistics and their own counts (Neumann 2022).

Considerations about what forms of violence are considered to be femicide are also inherent to defining and operationalizing femicide. Although intimate or sexual femicide is often emphasized in the literature, femicide is not a monolith and can refer to a broad set of violent acts ranging from the targeted killings of activists to unintended deaths due to female genital mutilation or forced abortions. Different documentation groups may intentionally or unintentionally focus on particular types of femicide and as a result measure the overarching phenomenon of femicide differently. Framing femicide as a repertoire of violence practices, rather than a singular form of violence, is a useful way to address some measurement challenges and allows for a richer study of femicidal violence. Many taxonomies of femicide already exist (e.g., EIGE 2021; Etherington and Baker 2015; Flores, César, and Salas 2010, 417; Monárrez 2010), but there remains a need for a taxonomy adapted to consider the specific types of femicide that occur in conflict, which may differ from those that occur in times of peace. Following Gutiérrez-Sanín and Wood (2017), for each specific form of femicide that is documented, we should also consider the frequency at which that form was used, the particular technique used, as well as whether the violence was targeted against specific social groups. This approach has been used to disambiguate different forms of sexual violence in armed conflict (Dumaine et al. 2021), and studies of femicide are likely to benefit from this approach as well.

Returning to the Guatemalan conflict, sexual femicide—or perhaps femigenocide (Segato 2014)—formed part of the repertoire of femicide used by government forces. These femicides were often perpetrated by members of the Army, primarily targeted against Mayan women and girls, and were widespread/systematic in nature (CEH. 1999; Leiby 2009; Cumes 2021). What other types of femicide formed part of the repertoires of violence used by the government forces? Did the repertoire change over time and were different forms of violence used in different places? How do these repertoires differ from those used by the paramilitaries or the guerrillas? Furthermore, do the patterns of femicide observed during the conflict differ from those pre- and post-conflict?[12] What are the underlying causal mechanisms driving these changes? The answers to these questions provide an opportunity to establish a more nuanced understanding of the impacts of femicide, as well as an opportunity for more precise comparisons of femicidal violence across time, space, perpetrators, and conflicts.

FOUR RECOMMENDATIONS FOR DATA COLLECTORS AND ANALYSTS

Despite the challenges associated with femicide data collection, the growing availability of quantitative data offers new opportunities to study patterns of violence, inform policies aimed at violence prevention, and further efforts to advance accountability and justice. To respond to these difficulties and produce the most rigorous quantitative analyses possible, the community of practice will need to adjust both data collection and data analysis methods.

Collect Contextual Information Regarding the Circumstances of the Killing Whenever Possible

Contextual information is critical for identifying and studying femicides—both in conflict and in peace—and databases documenting human rights abuses in conflict should be designed with these needs in mind. Gutiérrez-Sanín and Wood (2017) expand a provocation from Ball (1996) that offers a useful organizational framing for databases that aim to capture information to document patterns of violence in conflict in general: "Who did what to whom, and... how and how often?" (Gutiérrez-Sanín and Wood 2017, 26). The "who," "what," and "whom" elements capture information on three different units of analysis—the perpetrators(s), violent event(s), and victims(s)—which Walby et al. (2017) identify as essential components for capturing varying aspects of femicidal violence. The "how" and "how often" elements specifically support the documentation of repertoires of violence.

For databases documenting femicide, either alone or alongside other human rights abuses, this organizational practice should be complemented by additional contextual information to aid in distinguishing femicides

---

[12]For example, Morales Trujillo (2010) discusses how the Guatemalan conflict normalized a culture of violence such that many of the same forms of sexual violence (and femicide) have persisted even after peace accords were signed in 1996. Analyses comparing data on femicide pre-, during, and post-conflict could help clarify the enduring effects of conflict on femicide.

from other forms of lethal violence. Many different types and combinations of femicide-relevant variables have been suggested (e.g., Fumega 2019; Walby et al. 2017; Dawson and Carrigan 2021; EIGE 2021). Some examples of proposed contextual variables include: gender and sex of the victim, gender and sex of the perpetrator, relationship between the victim and the perpetrator, whether there is evidence of sexual violence, and whether the victim had previously denounced the perpetrator. Qualitative research should be used to help inform the selection of contextual variables to be included in the database (Weil 2017). This qualitative investigation is especially important if the dynamics of femicide in conflict differ from those observed in times of peace.

Collect Data in the Most Disaggregated Way Possible

The lack of universally accepted definitions and operationalizations of femicide make harmonizing data from different sources and drawing comparisons between the data collected by different organizations and in different contexts difficult. Collecting data with an emphasis on disaggregation would benefit efforts to harmonize data and facilitate comparisons between data sources. By "disaggregation," I mean that data should be collected in the most granular way possible. The European Institute for Gender Equality (EIGE; 2021) offers one example of a minimum set of variables that should be considered when documenting femicides in data systems. Their framework includes information on three levels of analysis—victims, perpetrators, and violent events—as suggested by Walby et al. (2017), and includes a substantial set of variables documenting the specific context of the killings, rather than lumping everything under the umbrellas of "female homicide" or "femicide" without noting potential differences.

One of the strengths of this approach is that it allows data users to identify cases that are consistent with their particular working definition of femicide or related to a specific form of femicide relevant to their analysis. Importantly, this does not require that everyone agree on a particular operationalization of femicide nor that everyone focuses on the same forms of femicide. Additionally, disaggregated data offers an opportunity to conduct sensitivity analyses on findings. By varying the criteria used to identify femicide cases (essentially recoding the data), the robustness of patterns of violence can be examined. One potential use case for this type of analysis would be to examine whether legal conceptualizations of violence are sufficiently covering the types of femicide being perpetrated. This information could then be used to help identify specific types of violence that have been overlooked by laws and policies. Returning to the example of Nicaragua, this is essentially what the feminist organizations did after the femicide law was changed. By continuing to collect data according to the original definition, they could identify that many femicides were occurring outside the context of existing intimate relationships and show how changes to the law impacted the government's reporting.

Use Data from Multiple Sources When Available

When multiple datasets documenting violence exist, they are likely to present different narratives about patterns of violence. This is true for conflict-related homicides generally, and femicides specifically, and can also be observed in times of peace (e.g., Suárez Val and Helena 2020; Tavera Fenollosa 2008). Some of these differences are likely attributable to differences in how femicide is measured, while others are due to the statistical biases that each dataset is subject to. What results is a "war of statistics": each dataset tells a different story about patterns of violence.[13] Selecting one source over another changes our understanding of the violence, which has implications for policy making, historical memory, and justice.

Rather than considering a single source, which is likely a convenience sample, to be the "truth," analysts should combine data from multiple sources. Each individual data source likely documents some (or many) unique cases that other data sources do not. Integrating these different data sources together, which would be easier if every source collected the same minimum information, helps provide a more complete understanding of the documented violence. While this combined dataset will still be missing information about victims whose stories were never documented—and thus not suitable for population-level inference—it is an important step toward accounting for missing data and calculating rigorous statistical estimates of patterns of violence.

Use Statistical Methods That Account for Missing Data When Conducting Analyses

Understanding patterns about missingness in femicide data is essential to answering questions about patterns of femicidal violence. Failing to account for missing data in our analyses risks incorrectly answering those questions. Multiple systems estimation (MSE; also known as capture-recapture in many disciplines) is one statistical method that could be applied to study femicides

---

[13]Tavera Fenollosa (2008) aptly uses this phrase (in Spanish) to describe the controversy that has emerged in Mexico, where every institution has its own interpretation of the impacts of femicide.

in armed conflict. In the context of lethal violence, MSE models use multiple incomplete lists of victims—like those that are emerging from femicide documentation efforts—in order to estimate the likely number of killings that were not documented by any of the sources. This method has previously been applied to study patterns of conflict-related homicides in other contexts (e.g., Lum et al. 2010; Hoover Green and Ball 2019; Rozo Ángel and Ball 2019), but has not yet been used to study femicide largely due to difficulty in obtaining data. As more and higher quality data on femicide becomes available, MSE has the potential to clarify crucial questions of fact necessary to understand the impacts of femicide.

MSE uses information about the documentation patterns of the recorded victims in order to make inferences about the size of the population that was never documented by any of the available sources.[14] For a documented killing, both the number of sources the victim appears on and specific pattern of documentation (e.g., the victim appeared on lists A and B, but not on list C) provide useful information used to estimate the size of the total victim population—both the femicides that have been documented and those that have not.[15] Estimating what is missing from available data allows us to draw more accurate conclusions about the patterns of violence and permits statistically valid comparisons. Additionally, the use of statistical models allows for the quantification of uncertainty around estimates, which yields more transparency about the range of plausible patterns of violence.

DISCUSSION

Studying statistical patterns of femicide, both in conflict and in peace, is difficult, but for all its challenges, the growing availability of quantitative data provides many opportunities to study key questions of fact that have previously gone unanswered. Related to policy, statistical analyses—

---

[14] For readers interested in learning more about MSE, Bird and King (2018) provide an overview of how MSE has previously been used to study human populations and inform public policy, Ball and Price (2018) provide an example of how MSE has previously been used for accountability efforts, and Chao (2001) provides a technical introduction to MSE models.

[15] MSE is one example of a statistical model capable of estimating the size of unknown victim populations that seems particularly appropriate for the current landscape of femicide data, but it is not the only method that can be used for these types of analyses. Retrospective mortality surveys (e.g., Silva and Ball 2006; Alburez-Gutierrez 2019) are another tool that has been used to study conflict-related mortality. Additionally, public health researchers often rely on excess deaths calculations, however these may prove challenging in conflict settings because accurate population measurements pre- and post-conflict are required.

particularly those that address the missing data issues present in femicide documentation—provide at least three distinct use cases. First, having robust statistics about the magnitude and scope of femicides makes the problem more difficult to ignore. Second, quantification allows for the identification of populations that are at higher risk for femicide perpetration or victimization. This is an important consideration for resource and service allocation, especially in settings where resources are heavily constrained. Finally, quantifying the problem allows for the evaluation of policies or interventions aimed at reducing violence. We cannot know if a policy is effective at reducing femicides if we do not understand the nature of the problem before and after the policy was implemented. As more data sources become available, we find ourselves closer to answers to these questions. Future quantitative research on femicide might consider the use of alternative data sources, such as digital trace data, the development of tools to facilitate femicide documentation (e.g., D'Ignazio et al. 2020), and the creation of statistical models to identify deficiencies in femicide registration.

Quantitative analyses, however, are not the only way of understanding femicide: they are part of a broader dialogue of approaches and are not a substitute for other types of analyses. The most powerful statistical analyses of patterns of femicide are likely to result from mixed methods work that relies on the strengths of both quantitative (e.g., generalizability and providing population-level context) and qualitative[16] (e.g., contextual understanding and case identification) approaches.

ACKNOWLEDGEMENTS

I would like to thank Dr. José Manuel Aburto, Dr. Patrick Ball, Hampton Gaddy, Dr. Megan Price, and the anonymous reviewer for their helpful comments on an earlier version. Any errors are my own.

ORCID

Maria Gargiulo http://orcid.org/0000-0003-1870-8990

RECOMMENDED READINGS

Alburez-Gutierrez, Diego. 2019. "Blood is Thicker than Bloodshed." *Demographic Research* 40:627–656. doi:10.4054/DemRes.2019.40.23.

Ball, Patrick. 1996. "Who Did What to Whom." In *Planning and Implementing a Large Scale Human Rights Data Project*. Washington, DC: American Association for the Advancement of Science (AAAS).

[16] See Weil (2017) for further discussion about the use of qualitative methods to study femicide.

Ball, Patrick, and Megan Price. 2018. "The Statistics of Genocide." *CHANCE* 31 (1): 38–45. doi:10.1080/09332480.2018.1438707.

Ball, Patrick, and Michael Reed. 2016. "El Registro y La Medición de La Criminalidad. El Problema de Los Datos Faltantes y El Uso de La Ciencia Para Producir Estimaciones En Relación Con El Homicidio En Colombia, Demostrado a Partir de Un Ejemplo: El Departamento de Antioquia (2003–2011)." *Revista Criminalidad* 58 (1):9–23.

Bird, Sheila M., and Ruth King. 2018. "Multiple Systems Estimation (or Capture-Recapture Estimation) to Inform Public Policy." *Annual Review of Statistics and Its Application* 5:95–118. doi:10.1146/annurev-statistics-031017-100641.

Carpenter, Dustin, Tova Fuller, and Les Roberts. 2013. "WikiLeaks and Iraq Body Count: The sum of parts may not add up to the whole–a comparison of two tallies of Iraqi civilian deaths." *Prehospital and Disaster Medicine* 28 (3):223–229. doi:10.1017/S1049023X13000113.

CEH. 1999. "*Guatemala: Memoria Del Silencio.*" *CEH* 8, vol. 2, 13–55. http://www.centrodememoriahistorica.gov.co/descargas/guatemalamemoria-silencio/guatemala-memoria-del-silencio.pdf.

Chao, Anne. 2001. "An Overview of Closed Capture-Recapture Models." *Journal of Agricultural, Biological, and Environmental Statistics* 6 (2):158–175. doi:10.1198/108571101750524670.

Corradi, Consuelo, Chaime Marcuello-Servós, Santiago Boira, and Shalva Weil. 2016. "Theories of Femicide and Their Significance for Social Research." *Current Sociology* 64 (7):975–995. doi:10.1177/0011392115622256.

Cumes, Aura Estela. 2021. "Sexual Violence in the Genocide of the Mayan People in Guatemala," in Federici Silvia, Mason-Deese Liz, and Draper Susana (eds.), *Feminicide and Global Accumulation: Frontline Struggles to Resist the Violence of Patriarchy and Capitalism*, 1st ed., 74–88. Brooklyn: Common Notions.

Dawkins, Sophia. 2021. "The Problem of the Missing Dead." *Journal of Peace Research* 58 (5):1098–1116. doi:10.1177/0022343320962159.

Dawson, Myrna, and Michelle Carrigan. 2021. "Identifying Femicide Locally and Globally: Understanding the Utility and Accessibility of Sex/Gender-Related Motives and Indicators." *Current Sociology* 69 (5):682–704. doi:10.1177/0011392120946359.

D'Ignazio, Catherine, and Lauren F. Klein. 2020. *Data feminism*. Cambridge, MA: MIT Press.

D'Ignazio, Catherine, Helena Suárez Val, Silvana Fumega, Harini Suresh, and Isadora Cruxên. 2020. "Feminicide & Machine Learning: Detecting Gender-Based Violence to Strengthen Civil Sector Activism." In *4th Workshop on Mechanism Design for Social Good*.

Driver, Alice. 2015. "More or Less Dead: Feminicide." *Haunting, and the Ethics of Representation in Mexico*. Tucson, AZ: University of Arizona Press.

Dumaine, Logan, Ragnhild Nordås, Maria Gargiulo, and Elisabeth Jean Wood. 2021. "Repertoires of Conflict-Related Sexual Violence: Introducing the RSVAC Data Package." *Journal of Peace Research*, November, 002234332110446. doi:10.1177/00223433211044674.

Economic Commission for Latin America and the Caribbean. 2014. "Annual Report 2013-2014: Confronting Violence against Women in Latin America and the Caribbean." LC/G.2626. Santiago: Chile.

Etherington, Nicole, and L. Baker. 2015. "Forms of Femicide." Learning Network Brief (29). London, Ontario: Learning Network, Centre for Research and Education on Violence Against Women and Children. http://www.vawlearningnetwork.ca.

European Institute for Gender Equality. 2021. "Measuring Femicide in the EU and Internationally: An Assessment." Lithuania: Publications Office. https://data.europa.eu/doi/10.2839/485134.

Flores, Fuentes, M. César, and Rubio Salas. 2010. *Violencia Contra Las Mujeres e Inseguridad Ciudadana En Ciudad Juárez*.

Fumega, Silvana. 2019. "Guía Para Protocolizar Procesos de Identificacion de Femicidios Para Su Posterior Registro." doi:10.5281/zenodo.1659628.

Grant, Emily, Lena Dechert, Laurel Wimbish, and Andria Blackwood. 2021. "Missing and Murdered Indigenous People: Statewide Report Wyoming." Wyoming Survey & Analysis Center. https://wysac.uwyo.edu/wysac/reports/View/7713.

Guberek, Tamy, Daniel Guzmán, Megan Price, Kristian Lum, and Patrick Ball. 2010. "To Count the Uncounted: An Estimation of Lethal Violence in Casanare." A Report by the Benetech Human Rights Program.

Gutiérrez-Sanín, Francisco, and Elisabeth Jean Wood. 2017. "What Should We Mean by 'Pattern of Political Violence'? Repertoire, Targeting, Frequency, and Technique." *Perspectives on Politics* 15 (1):20–41. doi:10.1017/S1537592716004114.

Hoover Green, Amelia, and Patrick Ball. 2019. "Civilian Killings and Disappearances During Civil War in El Salvador." *Demographic Research* 41:781–814. (1980–1992)." doi:10.4054/DemRes.2019.41.27.

Lagarde y de los Ríos, Marcela. 2010. "Preface: Feminist Keys for Understanding Feminicide." In *Terrorizing Women*, xi–xxvi. Durham, NC: Duke University Press.

Leiby, Michele L. 2009. "Wartime Sexual Violence in Guatemala and Peru." *International Studies Quarterly* 53 (2):445–468. doi:10.1111/j.1468-2478.2009.00541.x.

Lum, Kristian, Megan Price, Tamy Guberek, and Patrick Ball. 2010. "Measuring Elusive Populations with Bayesian Model Averaging for Multiple Systems Estimation: A Case Study on Lethal Violations in Casanare, 1998–2007." *Statistics, Politics, and Policy* 1 (1):1–29. doi:10.2202/2151-7509.1005.

Monárrez, Julia. 2010. "Las Diversas Representaciones Del Feminicidio y Los Asesinatos de Mujeres En Ciudad Juárez, 1993–2005." Violencia Contra Las Mujeres e Inseguridad Ciudadana En Ciudad Juárez 2.

Morales Trujillo, Hilda. 2010. "Femicide and Sexual Violence in Guatemala." In *Terrorizing Women: Feminicide in the Américas*, 127–137. Durham, NC: Duke University Press.

Neumann, Pamela. 2022. "'If It's Not Femicide, It's Still Murder': Contestations over Femicide in Nicaragua." *Feminist Criminology* 17 (1):139–159. doi:10.1177/15570851211037271.

Price, Megan. 2013. "Convenience Samples: What They Are, and What They Should (and Should Not) Be Used For." https://hrdag.org/2013/04/05/convenience-samples-what-they-are/.

Price, Megan, and Patrick Ball. 2014. "Big Data, Selection Bias, and the Statistical Patterns of Mortality in Conflict." *Sais Review of International Affairs* 34 (1):9–20. doi:10.1353/sais.2014.0010.

Radford, Jill, and DianaEH. Russell. 1992. *Femicide: The Politics of Woman Killing*. New York, NY: Twayne Publishers.

Rozo Ángel, Valentina, and Patrick Ball. 2019. "Asesinatos de Líderes Sociales En Colombia: Una Estimación Del Universo-Actualización 2018."

Segato, Rita Laura. 2014. "Las Nuevas Formas de La Guerra y El Cuerpo de Las Mujeres." *Sociedade e Estado* 29 (2):341–371. doi:10.1590/S0102-69922014000200003.

Silva, Romesh, and Patrick Donnell Ball. 2006. "*The Profile of Human Rights Violations in Timor-Leste*." Benetech Initiative.

Suárez Val, and Helena. 2020. "Datos Discordantes. Información Pública Sobre Femicidio En Uruguay."

Suárez Val, and Helena. 2021. "Feminicidio Uruguay." https://ohchr.org/Documents/Issues/Women/SR/Femicide/2021-submissions/CSOs/uruguay-feminicidio-1.pdf.

Tavera Fenollosa, Ligia. 2008. "Estadísticas Sobre Violencia de Género, Una Mirada Crítica Desde El Feminicidio." *Políticas Sociales y Género. Los Problemas Sociales y Metodológicos* 2:301–342.

Vargas, Theresa. 2022. "She's Spent Years Tracking the Killings of Black Women and Girls. Now, She's Planning a D.C. March." Washington Post, January 1, 2022. https://www.washingtonpost.com/dc-md-va/2022/01/01/black-women-girls-march-dc/.

Velasco, Karla. 2021. "Destabilizing Notions of Feminicide Victimhood: Disposable Lives and 'Ungrievable Deaths' of Sex Workers and Women Related to Narcos in Zacatecas, Mexico."

Walby, Sylvia, Jude Towers, Susie Balderston, Consuelo Corradi, Brian Francis, Markku Heiskanen, Karin Helweg-Larsen, et al. 2017. *The Concept and Measurement of Violence against Women and Men*. Bristol, UK: Policy Press.

Weil, Shalva. 2017. "The Advantages of Qualitative Research into Femicide." *Qualitative Sociology Review* 13 (3):118–125. doi:10.18778/1733-8077.13.3.08.

Invisible Police Lethal Violence against Black Women in the United States: An Intersectional Approach

JANICE JOSEPH

Over the past several years, police killings of Black men have received national and international attention. However, there is silence surrounding the deaths of Black women killed by the police. This paper examines the nature and extent of lethal police violence against Black women in the United States, Black women's vulnerability to police violence, and responses to their deaths. It also uses an intersectional approach to discuss why Black women face racialized and gendered police violence and how their deaths have been rendered invisible in public discourse and justice movements.

INVISIBILITY OF BLACK FEMALE VICTIMS OF POLICE LETHAL VIOLENCE IN THE UNITED STATES: AN INTERSECTIONAL APPROACH

Police violence is a leading cause of death for young men in the United States. Over the lifetime, about 1 in every 1,000 Black men can expect to be killed by police (Edwards, Lee, and Esposito 2019). Like Black men, Black women have experienced a long and painful history of police brutality in the United States. Due to their intersectional identities of race, gender, and class, Black women are one of the most vulnerable groups in the American society. Police violence against Black women seems to be a pervasive practice in an attempt to maintain the American hierarchical structure based on whiteness, maleness, and high socioeconomic status. Consequently, Black women lived experiences of police violence are shaped by the overlapping effects of racism, sexism, and classism. In addition, while police killings of several Black men have received a great of publicity, the police killings of Black women have remained invisible until recently. In order to contextualize police violence against Black women and the public responses to the killing of Black women, it is necessary provide an intersectional framework on how multiple forms of vulnerability predispose Black women to police violence and responses to their killings. This paper, therefore, uses an intersectional lens to examine Black women's vulnerability to police violence, the invisibility of their deaths, and attempts to highlight police fatal violence against them.

CONCEPT OF INTERSECTIONALITY

In 1989, Professor Kimberlé Crenshaw introduced the legal theory of intersectionality in her article *Demarginalizing the Intersection of Race and Sex: A Black Feminist Critique of Antidiscrimination Doctrine, Feminist Theory and Antiracist Politics.* In this article, Crenshaw illustrated how race and gender often interact to create multiple unique experiences for Black women in the workplace. She argued that Black women suffer discrimination resulting from a combination of both racism and sexism. This double discrimination against Black women results from the combined effects of race and gender and not the sum of race and gender discrimination. For the Black woman, gender and race are inextricably interlinked to create multidimensional forms of oppression and marginalization in the American society. Although intersectional approach has evolved to include factors such as sexual orientation, gender identity, religion, disability, physical appearance, the initial focus of the approach - Black women at the intersection of race and gender – is the basisof the discussion in this paper.

NATURE AND EXTENT OF POLICE KILLING OF BLACK WOMEN

There is a paucity of official data on the number of Black women killed by the police in the United States due to the fact that states seldom collect official data on the race of persons killed by the police. The killings of Blacks by the police are deprioritized by the official agencies that produce such official data. Consequently, most of the limited information on police violence against Black women is based on newspaper accounts, social media postings, research by scholars, and journalist reports (Jacobs 2017).

TABLE 1. Descriptive data of black women killed by police, 2003–2020.

N = 62	
Age	
18-24	37%
25-34	26%
35-44	13%
45-54	21%
55 and over	3%
How Killed	
Shot	95%
Other	5%
Victim with mental illness or mental crisis	
Yes	25%
No	75%
Regions Where Killed	
Northeast	13%
Midwest	16%
West	10%
South	61%

Sources: (Avanzar 2019; Chughtai 2020; Dzhanova et al. 2021; Gonzaga University 2020; Crenshaw et al. 2015).

A study conducted by Johnson, Gilbert, and Ibrahim (2018) indicates that unarmed Black women are most likely to be shot and killed by police than any other group, including Black men. Edwards, Lee, and Esposito (2019) report that Black women are 1.4 times more likely to be killed by police than are white women. According to Dzhanova et al. (2021), between February 2015 and March 2021, 50 Black women were shot and killed by the police. Since 2015, the *Washington Post* has created a database of every fatal shootings by an on-duty police officer in the United States. It provides data on police shootings by race, by gender, and the intersection of both race and gender. However, these data are limited because they exclude police killings by means other than shooting. The *Washington Post* data show that since 2015, nearly 250 women were shot and killed by officers over a period of five-year. Of these, twenty percent (48) were Black women, although they constitute 13 percent of the female population. The *Washington Post* also reported that 28% of the Black victims were unarmed. In addition, several Black women who were killed by police suffered from mental illness (Lati, Jenkins, and Brugal 2020) because Black women with mental health issues are particularly at risk for police violence (Jacobs 2017). It is quite clear that Black women are fatally shot at rates higher than women of other races.

Using information from the *Washington Post*, the *Insider* and cases from the internet, the author has created a profile of these Black women who were killed between 2003-2020 (see Table 1). The descriptive data in Table 1 show that the most of victims were young (between the age of

18-24), 95% were shot and 5% were suffocated, beaten to death or experienced brute force that caused their death. Most of the Black women was killed in the Southern region of the United States. Table 1 also indicates that 25 percent of the victims were mentally ill or experiencing a mental crisis at the time of their deaths.

One of the biggest failures of the criminal justice system in the United States is the lack of accountability or enforcement against police officers who kill Blacks. While fewer Black women than men are killed by the police, the conviction rate of the perpetrators is lower in those cases (Gupta 2020). Police misconduct trials are rare. Instead, cities pay millions to settle claims (Samuels, Mehta, and Wiederkehr 2021). Consequently, "law enforcement can erase the life of a Black woman with ease and very little accountability" (Jacobs 2017, 55).

INVISIBLE BLACK FEMALE VICTIMS OF POLICE VIOLENCE

Lack of Media Coverage and National Outrage

In recent years, the deaths of several Black males, such as George Floyd, Michael Brown, Eric Gardner, and many males have gained national publicity. However, the killings of Black women by police have been conspicuously absent from the media or receive very little attention during public conversations or discourse. "The stories of their deaths may be newsworthy, but the fact that the victim or survivor is a Black woman can be buried. There is a long-standing problem with media coverage, or the lack thereof, of crimes committed against Black women" (Jacobs 2017, 52). According to Crenshaw the common context to understanding police and state violence against Black people has largely focused on Black men. As a result, the exclusion of Black women remains prevalent (cited in Clifton 2015). "The erasure of Black women is not purely a matter of missing facts. Even where women and girls are present in the data, narratives framing police profiling and lethal force as exclusively male experiences lead researchers, the media, and advocates to exclude them" (Crenshaw et al. 2015, 4).

In addition, when the killings of Black women occurred during a news cycle that focuses on police violence against Blacks, they received far less publicity in comparison to the deaths of Black males (Crenshaw et al. 2015). This was evident in the case of Breonna Taylor whose death received far less national news coverage than George Floyd's murder which gained a great deal of publicity both nationally and internationally.

In the 60 days after Breonna Taylor's death, for example, there were only *eight articles* in the national media outlets that mentioned her name but George Floyd's name, by comparison, was mentioned in *22,046 articles* in the 60 days after he was murdered (Samuels, Mehta, and Wiederkehr 2021). A study conducted by Brown et al. (2017) of the Brookings Institution and the University of Maryland found that of the nearly 300 phrases used as Twitter hashtags between August 2014 and August 2015, a year after the killing of 18-year-old Michael Brown, none of the hashtags specifically mentioned a Black woman or girl; although there were at least ten Black women killed by police during that period (see Crenshaw et al. 2015).

The deaths of Black women also have not sparked the same level of national and global outrage against police brutality as the killing of several Black men by police officers. Two months before George Floyd was killed by police in Minneapolis, for example, Breonna Taylor was killed in her home in Louisville, Kentucky. Those officers who were alleged to have murdered George Floyd were terminated immediately from their employment and criminally charged but it took months for one officer in the Breonna Taylor's case to be terminated, charged and indicted. Her death received little media attention until the murder of George Floyd which generated major protests in the United States about police violence toward African Americans. In general, there has been no similar mobilized outrage for the killing of Black women by police in comparison to Black males; Breonna Taylor was the exception to the norm.

Most of the well published cases of Black males killed by police are often captured on video, thus these videos prompt immediate outrage. However, even when there were fatal shootings involving Black women that were captured by body camera footage, most still did receive extensive attention from the national media nor were there widespread protests. Instead, the outrage for the killing of Black females by police is seen as secondary, subordinate and inconsequential or is expressed as an afterthought (Cooper 2020; Martin 2021). This lack of attention to the killings of Black women by the police marginalizes, minimizes, and trivializes their lives and lived experiences of police abuse. This response also indirectly perpetuates "state-sponsored" violence against Black women's bodies and implies that Black women's lives are expendable.

Black Lives Matter Movement

The Black Lives Matter Movement was created in 2012 after the acquittal of George Zimmerman who killed Trayvon Martin. It has been at the forefront in the fight for racial justice. Its hashtag is an easy-to-remember slogan which has been a force in generating a new wave of civil rights protests and activism across the United States and around the world. The Black Lives Matter and the movement used 21st-century technology and social media, such as Twitter, Facebook and Tumblr to mobilize people fighting for social justice on the streets (Guynn 2015). This movement has become one of the most potent and effective activist movements for the Black population in the United States.

Over the years, the Black Lives Matter Movement has been strongly criticized because its activism has been centered almost exclusively on Black men, despite being founded by three women (Brown et al. 2017). Due to sexism, when Black women were killed, the Black Lives Matter's protests for these victims have been extremely small compared to those of Black men who were killed. "Because of the prioritization of Black men within the Black Lives Matter movement, Black women are again rendered invisible in the very reform movement originated to empower Black people. This disconnect fuels Black women's invisibility because they are not only silenced by police brutality, but also further sidelined within their own reform movements, regardless of subject matter" (Martin 2021, 1001).

The intersectional invisibility approach can be used to understand why Black women's experiences of police violence is often missing from the conversations and agenda of social justice movements. Black women, who are at the intersections of race and gender, are not fully recognized as members of their constituent groups (Purdie-Vaughns and Eibach 2008). The source of the intersectional invisibility is dual: as a woman, she is marginalized among women and as a Black person she is marginalized among Blacks because the prototypical woman is a White woman, and the prototypical Black person is a Black man (Coles and Pasek 2020). The Me Too Movement has often remained silent about police violence against Black women. Instead, it has been vocal about violence against middle- and upper-class white women, although it was created more than a decade ago by a Black woman (Morris 2020). Consequently, Black women are "at first victimized in raced and gendered ways by an apparatus of the state, then revictimized via neglect by the very movements that should aid them" (Coles and Pasek 2020, 2). As such they "tend to be marginalized members within marginalized groups. This status relegates them to a position of acute social invisibility" (Purdie-Vaughns and Eibach 2008, 181). When the deaths of Black men and White women overshadow the deaths of Black women, there is a tradeoff between sexism and racism, although the killings of Black women are affected by both forms of discrimination (Martin 2021). Consequently, the experiences of Black women become invisible relative to those of both White women and Black men and by the silence of their stories.

Because of criticisms, in recent years, the Black Lives Matter movement has been highlighting police brutality against Black women in the United States. However, Black women's experiences are still not given the same platform in the Black Lives Matter Movement in comparison to Black men's experiences (Martin 2021). It has become evident that Black women are forgotten and left behind in the movement which was intended to combat racism and empower Black people. More needs to be done by the Black Lives Matter Movement. It needs to fight for Black women because their lives matter as much as Black men lives matter.

SAY HER NAME CAMPAIGN

Say Her Name Campaign emerged as an alternate narrative to Black Lives Matter Movement. In 2014, *Say Her Name* Campaign was cofounded by Kimberlé Crenshaw and Luke Harris with the viral hashtag #SayHerName. It was in response to the blatant disparity between public recognition of Black men and Black women who are victimized by the police. #SayHerName is a catchy hashtag and it reminds the nation that Black women's lives matter also. It is a narrative that remembers and honors the lives of Black women (Borda and Marshall 2020).

This campaign is the initiative of the African American Policy Forum (AAPF) and Crenshaw views it as an avenue to raise awareness about the number of Black women who experienced police abuse and to bring their stories into the public debate. She also suggests that it is as a way of reclaiming the public dialogue in honor of Black women harmed and killed by police violence (Crenshaw 2020). It also highlights "Black women's experiences of police violence in an effort to support a gender-inclusive approach to racial justice that centers all Black lives equally" (Crenshaw et al. 2015, 1).

Using her concept of intersectionality, Crenshaw argues that Black women are rendered invisible and relegated to the margins of society because their identities lie at the intersections of race and gender (Bianco 2017). The goal of the movement is to serve "as a tool for the resurgent racial justice movement to mobilize around the stories of Black women who have lost their lives to police violence" (Crenshaw et al. 2015, 2).

In July 2015, following the death of Sandra Bland, who died in police custody in Waller County, Texas, Kimberlé Crenshaw and Andrea J. Ritchie along with Rachel Anspach, Rachel Gilmer and Luke Harris coauthored the report "Say Her Name: Resisting Police Brutality Against Black Women". The report was centered around Black women, most of whose deaths and other forms of police violence were missing from the public discourse on police violence and Blacks. The report identified Black female victims murdered by the police from 1984 to 2015. In addition, it detailed "not only these women's tragic deaths, but also the relational situations that called police to the scene, their deaths (often at home), and the behavioral health challenges that predominantly impact the treatment of Black women at the hands of police" (Borda and Marshall 2020, 134-135). According to Crenshaw et al. (2015), the authors' goal of the Say Her Name report is to illustrate the reality that Black women are killed and violated by police with alarming regularity. The authors hope "to call attention to the ways in which this reality is erased from our demonstrations, our discourse, and our demands to broaden our vision of social justice" (4).

In 2017, Andrea Ritchie published the book "Invisible No More: Police Violence Against Black Women and Women of Color" which focuses on the invisibility of Black women and women of color in the ongoing public dialogue surrounding the epidemic of police violence and brutality in the United States. She also highlighted the racial and gender biases within the American social system, especially the criminal justice system. Her book centers the women of color and those of sexual orientation and explores the various forms of police violence they experience and have gone unnoticed. It is timely examination of the present discourse on Black women and police abuse.

CONCLUSION

Although the tragic killings of Black men have been the impetus for mass protests, rallies, and verbal discourse on police violence against the Black community, Black female victims of such abuse have been forgotten. Black women should no longer be overlooked in public conversations about racism, sexism and police violence. They should also become the focal point of mass social justice movements and public discourse. Centering their experiences of police violence will ensure that their stories are heard. Their experiences with police violence should no longer be considered peripheral and anecdotal. The amplification of their deaths is critical to the elimination of the racialized and gendered violence that they experience at the hands of the American police. To eliminate the shroud of silence and invisibility that surround police killings of Black women, an intersectional prism is needed for a more inclusive and expansive examination of police violence in the Black community. Bringing visibility to police violence against Black women will be a form of social justice for these victims.

According to Crenshaw et al. (2015):

> "When the lives of marginalized Black women are centered, a clearer picture of structural oppressions emerges. No analysis of state violence against Black bodies can be complete without including all Black bodies within its frame. Until we say the names and tell the stories of the entire Black community, we cannot truly claim to fight for all Black lives" (30).

RECOMMENDED READINGS

Avanzar. 2019. "Safety, Justice, Empowerment." https://avanzarnow.org/did-you-know/

Bianco, Marcie. 2017. "Kimberlé Crenshaw Delivers an Exceptional Jing Lyman Lecture." https://gender.stanford.edu/news-publications/gender-news/kimberl-crenshaw-delivers-exceptional-jing-lyman-lecture

Borda, Jennifer, L., and Bailey Marshall. 2020. "Creating a Space to #SayHerName: Rhetorical Stratification in the Networked Sphere." *Quarterly Journal of Speech* 106 (2):133–155. doi:10.1080/00335630.2020.1744182.

Brown, Melissa, and Rashawn Ray, Ed Summers, and Neil Fraistat. 2017. "#SayHerName: A Case Study of Intersectional Social Media Activism." *Ethnic and Racial Studies* 40 (11):1831–1846. doi:10.1080/01419870.2017.1334934.

Chughtai, Alia. 2020. "Know Their Names: Black People Killed by the Police in the US." https://interactive.aljazeera.com/aje/2020/know-their-names/index.html

Clifton, Derrick. 2015. "Impact." https://www.mic.com/articles/117228/black-women-continue-getting-killed-by-police-why-aren-t-more-people-discussing-it

Coles, Stewart, and Josh Pasek. 2020. "Intersectional Invisibility Revisited: How Group Prototypes Lead to the Erasure and Exclusion of Black Women." *Translational Issues in Psychological Science* 6 (4):314–324. doi:10.1037/tps0000256.

Collins, Patricia Hill. 2000. *Black Feminist Thought: Knowledge, Consciousness, and the Politics of Empowerment*. Abingdon: Routledge.

Cooper, Brittney. 2020. "Why Are Black Women and Girls Still an Afterthought in Our Outrage Over Police Violence?" *Time*. https://time.com/5847970/police-brutality-black-women-girls/

Crenshaw, Kimberlé, Andrea J. Richie, Rachel Anspach, Rachel Gilme, and Luke Harris. 2015. *Say Her Name: Resisting Police Brutality against Black Women*. New York: African American Policy Forum.

Crenshaw, Kimberlé. 1989. *Demarginalizing the Intersection of Race and Sex: A Black Feminist Critique of Antidiscrimination Doctrine. Feminist Theory and Antiracist Politics*. University of Chicago Legal Forum, Vol. 1989, no. 1, 139–167. Article 8. https://chicagounbound.uchicago.edu/cgi/viewcontent.cgi?article=1052&context=uclf

Crenshaw, Kimberlé. 2020. "Naming the Threat: The Scourge of Police Violence Targeting Black Women." *The New Republic*. https://newrepublic.com/article/156011/naming-threat

Dukes, Kristin Nicole, and Sarah E. Gaither. 2017. "Black Racial Stereotypes and Victim Blaming: Implications for Media Coverage and Criminal Proceedings in Cases of Police Violence against Racial and Ethnic Minorities." *Journal of Social Issues* 73 (4): 789–807. doi:10.1111/josi.12248.

Dzhanova, Yelena, Taylor Ardrey, Ellen Cranley, Hannah Beckler, and Bre'Anna Grant. 2021. "50 Black Women Have Been Killed by US Police since 2015. No One of the Officers Has Been Convicted." *Insider*. https://www.insider.com/black-women-killed-by-police-database-2021-6

Edwards, Frank, Hedwig Lee, and Michael Esposito. 2019. "Risk of Being Killed by Police Use of Force in the United States by Age, Race-Ethnicity, and Sex." *Proceedings of the National Academy of Sciences of the United States of America* 116 (34):16793–16798. . . doi:10.1073/pnas.1821204116.

Gonzaga University. 2020. "Say Their Name." https://www.gonzaga.edu/about/offices-services/diversity-inclusion-community-equity/say-their-name.

Gupta, Alisha Haridasani. 2020. "Since 2015: 48 Black Women Killed by the Police. And Only 2 Charges." *The New York Times*. https://www.nytimes.com/2020/09/24/us/breonna-taylor-grand-jury-black-women.html

Guynn, Jessica. 2015. "Meet the Woman Who Coined #BlackLivesMatter." *USA Today*. http://www.usatoday.com/story/tech/2015/03/04/alicia-garza-black-lives-matter/24341593

Jacobs, Michelle S. 2017. "The Violent State: Black Women's Invisible Struggle against Police Violence." *William. & Mary Journal of Women & Law* 24 (4):39–100. https://scholarship.law.wm.edu/wmjowl/vol24/iss1/4.

Johnson, Odis, Keon Gilbert, and Habiba Ibrahim. 2018. *Race, Gender and the Contexts of Unarmed Fatal Interactions with Police*. St. Louis, MO: Washington University. https://cpb-us-w2.wpmucdn.com/sites.wustl.edu/dist/b/1205/files/2018/02/Race-Gender-and-Unarmed-1y9md6e.pdf.

Lati, Marisa, Jennifer Jenkins, and Sommer Brugal. 2020. "Nearly 250 Women Have Been Fatally Shot by Police since 2015." *Washington Post*. file:///G:/Nearly%20250%20women%20have%20been%20fatally%20shot%20by%20police%20since%202015%20-%20Washington%20Post.htm

Martin, Jordon. 2021. "Breonna Taylor: Transforming a Hashtag into Defunding the Police." *The Journal of Criminal Law and Criminology* 111 (4):995–1030.

Morris, Kadish. 2020. "Tarana Burke: 'If It Weren't for Black Women, I would Not Have Made It." *The Guardian*. https://www.theguardian.com/us-news/2020/nov/15/tarana-burke-if-it-werent-for-black-women-i-would-not-have-made-it

Purdie-Vaughns, Valerie, and Richard P. Eibach. 2008. "Intersectional Invisibility: The Distinctive Advantages and Disadvantages of Multiple Subordinate-Group Identities." *Sex Roles* 59 (5–6):377–391. https://doi.org/10.1007/s11199-008-9424-42. doi:10.1007/s11199-008-9424-4.

Ritchie, Andrea J. 2017. *Invisible No More: Police Violence against Black Women and Women of Color*. Boston, MA: Beacon Press.

Samuels, Alex, Dhrumil Mehta, and Anna Wiederkehr. 2021. "Why Black Women Are Often Missing From Conversations About Police Violence." *FiveThirtyEight*. https://fivethirtyeight.com/features/why-black-women-are-often-missing-from-conversations-about-police-violence/

Understanding and Addressing Femicide in Peacetime Zimbabwe

Kudakwashe Chirambwi

INTRODUCTION

It is essential to research femicide in Zimbabwe not only because it is one of the most extreme forms of violence against women, but the typologies and circumstances that lead to this killing continue to escape policy and scholarly attention. Secular and religious institutions in Zimbabwe entrench gender stereotypes and constructions of masculinity that emphasize power, violence, and dominance (Keith, Fran, and Robyn 2022). There is a plethora of literature concurring that "custom in Africa is stronger than domination, stronger than the law, stronger even than religion." Over the years, customary practices have been incorporated into religion and ultimately have come to be believed by their practitioners to be demanded by their adopted gods, whomever they may be (Lightfoot-Klein 1989, 47). As such, the patriarchal customs assign gender roles that perpetuate male aggression and perpetuate structures based on hierarchy, violence, and humiliation that result in femicide. This view is corroborated by Iranzo's (2015, 1) view that femicide is:

> the killing of a woman because some man or men, although occasionally also some women who accept men's values, has or have sentenced her to death adducing whatever reasons, motives or causes, but nonetheless actually and ultimately because he or they believe she has defied (the words they often use are 'offended' or 'insulted') patriarchal order (in their words' honourable' societies) beyond what her judge (often but not always the same person who kills her) is prepared to tolerate without retaliating in that way.

Zimbabwe is not far from the observations made in the first anthology on femicide by Radford (1992, 3) that femicide occurs "in the context of the overall oppression of women in a patriarchal society" characterized by "misogynous killing of women by men."

Because of the misogynist tendencies embedded in the cultural norms undergirding male-female interactions (Zimbabwe Cultural Atlas 2022), as observed by Standish and Weil (2021, 812), femicide then carries a "special nuance" as "it is the intentional murder of women because they are women." Zimbabwe is a patriarchal society with diverse aspects of misogyny, as men combine patriarchy, gynophobia, and phallocentrism ideology to perpetrate violence against women (Mukumana et al. 2020). Phallocentrism is the ideology that the male sexual organ is the central element in the organization of the social world – resulting in masculine power and dominance.

As revealed by interviewees, family femicide occurs primarily due to three fundamental addictions by Zimbabwean men: love of wealth, power, and honor—any challenge of these results in fatal outcomes. Women are killed by male elders of their families (fathers, uncles, and brothers) for bringing shame, primarily through rape and witchcraft, or sorcery (Miguel 2005). Husbands also kill their wives for dishonoring them and their clan for engaging in flirtation and illicit affairs. Love of honor is usually premised on the a priori assumption that the father is the head of the family, therefore superior to women.

Zimbabwe is a landlocked country covering an area of 390,757km2. The UN estimates the population to be at 15,092,171, of which the female population amounts to approximately 7.77 million, and 7 322 172 are male. As such, femicide has become an epidemic that threatens more than half of the total population. Despite recent advancements in the law and national campaigns to address violence, Zimbabwe still bleakly ranks 126 in the Gender Inequality Index and 56 in Global Gender Gap Index (UN Women 2021). The lifetime physical violence sits at 37.6%. However, the official national statistics on femicide are not available, despite the practice increasingly being widespread, as shown by electronic media.

This is consistent with research findings from western countries, that "to this day, in most countries, femicide statistics are still part of homicide data, which is part of the problem and the way the social order legitimizes or even tolerates the killings of women because of their gender" (Standish and Weil 2021, 812). Although the International Classification of Crime for Statistical Purposes provides the framework for recording femicide and gender-related crime data, based on the situational context, geographical location, date, time, and motive, this data is not readily available in Zimbabwe (UNODC 2018).

Femicide discourse is not visible in the criminal justice system (possibly a denial in using the concept). The statistics from the police and courts are staggering due to institutional and practical barriers. Research evidence shows that legal and procedural practice do not aggregate data, separating homicide from femicide, making it challenging to interpret incremental trends of the murder of women meaningfully. The absence of disaggregated data on forms and nature of femicide has undermined efforts to understand the geographic spread and magnitude of the murder of women. Research findings reveal that women in Zimbabwe are subjected to entrenched patriarchal and intimate partner femicides due to their subordinate position within the home. In equal measure, they all suffer from political and stranger femicides – killings that are random or targeted and often include sexual violence.

Further evidence shows that structurally, patriarchy, fractured relationships, reversal of gender roles, financial stress, high male unemployment, food insecurity, drug, and alcohol abuse intersected in instigating all forms of femicide. For instance, there has been a sharp spike in Covid-19 induced femicide, especially between 2020 and 2021, when most women were forced to shelter-in-place (Weil et al. 2018, Weil 2020, Standish 2021, Standish and Weil 2021). This is attributed to high household stress caused by financial pressures due to Covid-19 induced job cuts and lack of social support networks. Therefore, the enduring questions guiding this analysis are: What would femicide in Zimbabwe consist of? What are the gaps, and what examples are there as the potential for interventions?

METHODOLOGY

The study was a cross-sectional study in 10 provinces of Zimbabwe where all forms of femicide have significantly increased. A fieldwork study was carried out between 1 January 2020 and 17 December 2021. The study was designed as a retrospective, with data collected from a random sample of 251 participants. Of these respondents, 40 males and 50 female police officers were interviewed, particularly those serving in the homicide and Victim Friendly Unit sections. It emerged that the crime management system did not use the term femicide, and they also don't have the provision for capturing familial relationships leading to femicide. Since the police work hand in glove with magistrates and prosecutors, it was imperative to hear the latter's views on what motivates femicides and how they have legally categorized and interpreted them. To achieve this, nine female and 17 male judges, as well as 16 male and 14 female prosecutors, were consulted through either telephonic or face-to-face in-depth interviews. Views and examples from in-depth interviews with the criminal justice systems were followed up by reviewing police dockets and court decisions. It was imperative to have a conversation with victims' families to deepen understanding of the manifestations of intimate femicide, family member femicide, and political femicide.

As such, nine focus group discussions were carried out. The composition was determined by the family setup, but the majority had an equal number of male and female representatives of not more than 10 participants per group. However, a face-to-face conversation was held with 40 females and 32 male relatives of victims. In cases where the victim's family was in the diaspora, remote research, particularly in-depth interviews via Zoom and Skype platforms, was relied upon. Of these, six family members were interviewed. To examine the efficacy of peace institutions (known as chapter 12 institutions in Zimbabwe), the researcher interviewed two male Commissioners from the National Peace and Reconciliation Commission, three females from the Zimbabwe Gender Commission, and four females from the Zimbabwe Human Rights Commission.

A desk review was used to access official documents produced by different international and regional organizations to construct the cause and effects of femicide. These documents include press statements, meeting communiqués, agendas and records, reports, declarations, protocols, agreements, Memoranda, and other introductory framework texts by the Southern African Development Community, African Union, and United Nations. These policy papers were perused to understand the commitments and positions of various actors and political leaders on femicide. What further emerged is the disturbing level of disquiet about femicide. Access to these institutions is a significant issue, particularly to rural women. It is worrisome that institutions established for gender justice are not known and used by the people who are supposed to use them.

Gray literature and interviews revealed different typologies of femicide and institutional and structural motivators. See Table 1, showing typologies of femicide and the rates of prevalence.

Research findings show that intimate partner and stranger violence are strongly associated with femicide in Zimbabwe, and their prevalence is continuing unabated. Of the recorded incidences, 43.47% were killed by an intimate partner, 26.53% were murdered by strangers or unknown partners, 24.29% were murdered by family members, and 5.71% died from political violence. These are accounted for by a culture of machismo that fosters norms that facilitate misogynist tendencies among Zimbabwean men. The fatality distribution by province shows that the mining area of Midlands has the highest prevalence (15.78%), followed by the border area of Matebeleland South (12,79%), and then the

TABLE 1. Typologies and prevalence of Femicide.

Femicide occurrences in Zimbabwe Province	Aug. 2020 Forms of femicide				Dec. 2021 Forms of femicide			
	IPF	SF	FMF	PF	IPF	SF	FMF	PF
Harare	25	16	20	4	40	10	41	2
Bulawayo	30	20	17	3	43	20	18	1
Manicaland	17	19	16	4	36	17	17	4
Mashonaland Central	20	18	16	5	41	13	19	3
Mashonaland East	17	12	10	2	26	19	13	2
Mashonaland West	27	14	14	6	38	21	28	4
Midlands	34	32	21	13	44	40	32	16
Masvingo	16	10	9	2	23	14	12	3
Matebeleland North	33	19	12	1	41	14	11	2
Matebeleland South	40	22	16	3	48	40	15	4
Total	259	182	151	43	380	208	206	41
Grand Total		635				835		

KeyIPF – Intimate-partner femicide, SF – Stranger femicide, FF – Family member femicide, PF – Political femicide

TABLE 2. Rate of femicide in cases 2020 and 2021.

Femicide occurrences in Zimbabwe Province	Percentage Increase From 2020 to 2021			
	IPF	SF	FMF	PF
Harare	60%	−38%	105%	−50%
Bulawayo	43%	0%	6%	−67%
Manicaland	112%	−11%	6%	0%
Mashonaland Central	105%	−28%	19%	−40%
Mashonaland East	53%	58%	30%	0%
Mashonaland West	41%	50%	100%	−33%
Midlands	29%	25%	52%	23%
Masvingo	44%	40%	33%	50%
Matebeleland North	24%	−26%	−8%	100%
Matebeleland South	20%	82%	−6%	33%
Total	47%	14%	36%	−5%
Grand Total		31%		

populous capital city Harare (10.75%). The least murder rates have occurred in a small province like Masvingo (6.05%) and Mashonaland East (6.87%).

The evidence further shows a significant increase in the rate of femicide cases in-between the years 2020 and 2021. For instance, intimate partner femicide increased by 47%, stranger femicide soared up by 14%, family member femicide skyrocketed by 36%, and political femicide declined by 5%—Table 2 the variations in increases per province.

The increases are attributed to financial constraints that have been exacerbated by multi-dimensional challenges brought in by Covid-19. During the pandemic lockdown, domestic violence leading to femicide increased – to the extent of being popularized as "shadow pandemic."

However, grasping the overarching prevalence of femicide is difficult in Zimbabwe. This is due to a lack of centralized statistics, especially national-level data, national registries, or dedicated sections that capture incidents and types of femicide. The police statistics are equally challenging, as they have a tendency of under-reporting of forms of violence.

Theoretically, the research required the investigator to adopt an intersection conceptual framework to avoid homogenizing women, types of murder, and barriers to femicide interventions (Claire et al. 2013, Marieke and Koenraadt 2018). Intersectional theory, which heavily draws from feminist theory, seeks to explain the different layers of femicide and the multiplicity of systems that produce it, including power relations, politics, the proliferation of firearms, and socioeconomic status. According to this theory, it would be simplistic to reduce femicide to homicide since different women suffer interconnecting forms of gendered killing.

CONCEPTUALIZING FEMICIDE

There is a lack of a standardized definition of femicide among the police, magistrate, prosecutors, and civil society organizations (Weil 2016). Research evidence shows that domestic or intimate partner femicide is generally under-captured in police and court records as "assault" or "assault with intent to cause grievous bodily harm," "attempted murder" or "homicide" (Campbell and Runyan 1998, Corradi et al. 2016, Medie and Alice 2018, Medie 2018, 2019). In Zimbabwe, femicide is broadly criminalized by the criminal justice system as homicide – not as a separate criminal offense. A police interviewee, for example, stated that they code and operationalize femicide using the concept or indicator of "female victims of homicide" especially instigated by intimate partners or strangers – not as femicide per se. The police's challenges are corroborated by scholarly observations that one of the weaknesses of femicide is operational. For example, Corradi et al. (2016, 6) questioned, how can we capture the misogynist motivation, the assumption that this particular woman was murdered, 'simply because she is a woman'? We either assume that the mere fact of belonging to the female gender makes any woman a potential victim – however, this would amount to a very generic hypothesis with little empirical significance; or we demand further details on the perpetrator's motives, his relationship with the victim and the circumstances of the event.

Further, codes of "family homicides" or "domestic homicides" are used to refer to murder by an intimate partner or family member (Marcuello-Servós et al. 2016). Rarely do you hear the police and magistrates using specific terms such as "uxoricide" to refer to female victims, such as killing an intimate female partner, or "mariticide" to denote male victims (Dawson 2016). This is problematic. Such conceptualization misinterprets and underestimates the level of crime as it represents almost an equal share of male and female victims. It means all forms of femicide fall under the definition of homicide, which refers to killing one person by another.

The immediate implication is that the police and courts follow the same pattern of investigations as other homicide offenses. One of the prosecutors pointed out, "at the moment, there are no additional legislative provisions specifically for prosecuting femicide." However, the crime differs from male homicide in specific ways. The interviews revealed a lack of specialization in gender-based femicide, undermining the criminal justice system's gendered perspective in femicide cases. The police and prosecutors cited lack of resources, heavy workloads, and inadequate equipment as significant obstacles to legal accountability for femicide. It is problematic that individual police officers and victims' family members buy materials, such as photo equipment, paper, and cotton swabs for investigations and autopsies. As such, it is complicated to quantify whether the levels of prosecution or convictions are adequate responses to femicide. It is not clear the impact of criminal justice in deterring recurrence for those convicted.

The use of the term homicide is organically problematic. The noun homicide is derived from the Latin word, "homo," meaning man, and "cida," referring to killing. So homicide means killing a man. It is not clear how it includes women. As Jill and Russell (1992) observed, femicide is most preferred because it "would help remove the obscuring veil" of male-biased terms such as "homicide" and "manslaughter." The nomenclature femicide was first publicly introduced by Diana Russell while testifying about murders of women at the International Tribunal on Crimes Against Women in Brussels in 1976 (Radford and Russell 1992). In 1992, Russell and Jill defined femicide as "the misogynistic killing of women by men." In subsequent years, other authors such as Campbell and Runyan refined and broadened the definition to include "all killings of women, regardless of motive or perpetrator status." In the same year 1992, the first anthology on femicide redefined the practice as "the misogynous killing of women by men motivated by hatred, contempt, pleasure, or a sense of ownership over women, rooted in historically unequal power relations between women and men" (Caputi and Russell 1990). In subsequent years, Russell (2011, 3) chose the new term "femicide to refer to the killing of females by males because they are female" to demonstrate the magnitude of misogyny. However, scholars such as Johansson (2021, 26) counter-argued Russel's dominant conceptualization by observing that:

> femicide, with its portrayal of misogyny and holding male perpetrators attributable, is not sufficient to see the bigger picture. Rather, it has been discussed that by reviewing the structures of society, the term feminicide can be of service to reveal societal structures, including the attributes of the judicial system and the state as such, that normalize inequity, sexism, and misogyny.

While such scholarly definitions are limited to murders of females by males, research findings in Zimbabwe challenge the exclusion of female perpetrators and suggest a maximalist conception that captures extended femicide or covert femicide. This includes female-to-female murders. In Zimbabwe, some women are agents of patriarchy, and others act as agents of drug perpetrators and even on their own behalf as robbers. They facilitate the death of other women. Such incidents are among many covert forms of femicide, including botched abortions, hysterectomies. and genital mutilation, traditional practices where young females are married to much older men. For instance, Zimbabwe has one of the highest HIV and AIDS prevalence rates globally, with 20.1 percent of the population infected with the disease. Women are more affected by HIV than men, with 36 percent of women in the 17–50-year age group being infected. This is due to male in domination, sexism, and rape – resulting in mass femicide, often ignored by the criminal justice system.

Femicide is not presently recognized as such by the law. Zimbabwe has several laws and policies that aim to address GBV, but there is no solid evidence base specifically for femicide. Some of the progressive laws and policies include the Domestic Violence Act, 116 of 1998 (DVA) and the Criminal Law Codification and Reform Act (Sexual Offenses and Related Matters) Amendment Act, 32 of 2007 (Sexual Offenses Act). However, for instance, although the DVA has an expansive definition of domestic violence that includes physical, sexual, emotional, verbal, psychological, and economic abuse and intimidation, harassment, stalking, and controlling behaviors, it hardly mentions femicide. The following sections examine the manifestation of femicide in Zimbabwe and the implications to policy.

The killing of women in Zimbabwe because of their gender takes several dimensions but can be narrowed into four categories for analytical purposes. The following section explores the variations and how they intersect and interact at multiple levels. Drawing from the ecological intersection framework, femicide occurs at the interpersonal level (intimate partner femicide – for example, murder by husbands/ex-husbands, lovers/ex-lovers, sex partners, boyfriends/ex-boyfriends). It also happens at the microsystem level (family femicide), where it is "perpetrated by family members, the most predominant form being so-called 'honor killings'. Partners typically carry out these murders, brothers, fathers, or even hired assassins to protect against what is perceived as "shame" brought upon the family by the victim" (Standish and Weil 2021, 812). Another variation happens at the exosystem level (political femicide) – for example, at a national political level where women are taken as a "weapon of war" to persecute rivalry political parties). The last occurs at the macrosystem (covert femicide), such as HIV/AIDS. Possibly this pervasiveness could be the reason which compelled Weil (2020, 1) to view femicide as a shadow pandemic, as she concluded that "femicide, like the coronavirus, occurs in every society indiscriminately and spreads at an incalculable rate."

INTIMATE PARTNER FEMICIDE

The majority of families of victims of intimate partner femicide concurred that often, the murder precedes a lengthy history of abuse of a woman (Weil 2020). In most cases, these victims sometimes protect their abusers because they fear them. Also, the shame that comes with it from the African society makes many women not to speak up. These precursors were not captured in the criminal justice system records. Further evidence revealed that most fatalities were perpetrated by husbands and ex-husbands, followed by cohabiting partners (boyfriends) and then ex-boyfriends. Below, Table 3 shows selected husband-related femicide, the circumstance of murder, and the method used as recorded by media platforms between August–December 2021 only.

TABLE 3. Husband related Femicide.

Publisher	Type of partner	Incident-title	Method of killing	Date/Year
The Chronicle and police report https://www.chronicle.co.zw/listen-intimate-partner-violence-has-bulawayo-police-worried/.	Husband	Killed wife after a misunderstanding,	Sticks and logs, the body was thrown in a disused mine	August 29 2021
The Chronicle and police report https://www.chronicle.co.zw/listen-intimate-partner-violence-has-bulawayo-police-worried/.	Husband	Wife killed for suspected infidelity	Thrown through the window of high-rise apartment	September 15 2021
ZWNEWS	Ex-husband	Ex-boyfriend(45) kills woman(20) in front of husband(29)	Stabbed using okapi knife	December 7 2021
The Chronicle	Husband	Here lies wife, children killer, and prayer warrior	Knife and ax	November 10 2021
The Chronicle	Husband	Man commits suicide after killing wife in an infidelity row	Strangled	December 17 2021

In these incidents, a consistent pattern is of husbands' desire for power, dominance, and control over women emerges, in what López (2019) considers as an androcentric unconscious that permeates all patriarchal societies. Hence, the need to understand this crime as the intersection or interaction of relational vulnerability of women and patriarchal influence. The act of killing a wife is construed as maintaining control over her, with it being better than losing her to another man.

The fatalities exponentially increased in 2021 because male intimate partners have taken advantage of the secrecy and isolation brought by Covid-19 lockdown measures (Weil 2020, Standish and Weil 2021). Women may have been unable to venture out because either they lacked a valid excuse, or because they were afraid of being confronted by police or were fearful of getting Covid-19, bringing the virus home, and infecting their children. This may have meant that women could not report their cases because they could not get to a police station and could not go to court to get orders under the Domestic Violence Act. The majority of femicide incidents occur in the private sphere, such as the house occupied by the perpetrator and the victim, the house of the victim, or the perpetrator's house.

As a female interviewee stated, "such fatalities happen as if Zimbabwe is in wartime, yet most often, murder of wives happens within the home and at the hands of their husbands. We would expect divorced and separated women and husbands who are in conflict to have a high percentage of murders, not married women in their homes." What is emerging here is that the factors motivating femicide are unknown, as evidence shows that most of the murders were premeditated. Many factors intersect in the same incident, as motives are heterogeneous and complex to identify precisely. Initially, the reasons appear to be crimes of passion mostly related to an intense relationship that went terribly wrong; but also appear as if the murders were motivated by family problems involving ruminative thinking over economic challenges such as insurmountable debts and unemployment.

Another version of intimate partner femicide emerging from Zimbabwe is femicide by family members, located at the intersections of patriarchy and honor, especially in the male-dominated Zimbabwean communities. In both secular and religious practices, Zimbabwe is a heavily patriarchal society in urban and rural settings, where men have a sense of entitlement over women (Kambarami 2006, Zengenene 2019). Elsewhere, the research findings by Henrik et al. (2012, 45) revealed that the planning and execution of femicide "often involve multiple family members, usually without personality disorders or major mental disorders, and can include mothers, sisters, brothers, male cousins, uncles and grandfathers whose actions are by many, themselves included, considered as good or necessary." The intersections of patriarchy and intimate partner and familial partner femicides can be drawn. The attitudes toward killings are influenced by collectivist cultures, where:

> female morality is imposed through the constant disciplining of women's bodies (clothes, hair, manners, etc.), which becomes a type of symbolic confinement reassured by culture, always determined and conditioned by the male gaze, either for pleasure or incitement (Méndez and Barraza 2022, 17).

STRANGER FEMICIDE

Intimate partner femicide is somehow counterbalanced with high levels of stranger femicides, popularized as non-intimate partner femicides. For instance, Zimbabwe has experienced an exponential rise of organized crime-related femicide, involving murder associated with gangs, drug dealing, human trafficking, and ritual murders. Not much is known about femicide in the context of organized crime involving drug dealing, gangs, massive migration and human and drug trafficking chains. As Zimbabwe is experiencing an economic downturn, women are pressured to be involved in illegal markets which are at significant risk from organized crime. Research findings reveal a high prevalence of non-intimate femicide in sex workers, who are forced to operate in highly criminal environments. Most female sex workers are killed by their clients over appropriate fees paid for the sexual service. Others are murdered during the violence, robbery, and other high-risk behaviors.

A significant proportion of Zimbabwean men are in possession of legal and illegal firearms, and a lot of unemployed men are increasingly having problems with alcohol and drugs. Zimbabwe is increasingly becoming one of the most violent societies. There are several intersections here. The woman was part of a male gang. As a woman, she was overkilled, implying that the attack was excessive. A female respondent had the view that, among other reasons, "possibly, the association between guns and men has been inherited from the war of the liberation struggle (1969–1980) where gun use was valued and encouraged as a means to solve conflicts." Her views are buttressed by Kirsten's (Adèle 2007) observation that "males own most firearms–whether in state structures such as the police or military, as part of non-state armed groups, gangs, and militias, for leisure or sporting activities such as hunting, or for self-defense in the home" putting women at significant risk of being shot at.

What emerged from interviews, which is absent in literature and the criminal justice system, is political femicide. The following section explores this classification of femicide and how it intersects with other typologies.

POLITICAL FEMICIDE

The availability of data on political femicide is minimal, possibly because of the nature of domestic politics and circumstances motivating the murder. In political femicide, it is challenging to identify the perpetrator, a problem similar to open conflict situations. Zimbabwe has had a long history of conflict. Women's bodies are essentially an extension of the political battlefield. As such, there has been social and political acceptance of violence to solve conflicts. Méndez and Barraza(2022, 24) concur that "the use of violence, as an instrument and as a means to communicate, has a well-documented history in the sociology and psychology of social control and dominance." An elderly female respondent whose daughter was murdered during politically motivated violence opined that "the increased risk of violence for women is rooted in colonial political values that continued post-independence." Historical records show that acts of femicide were perpetrated by armed actors – colonial troops and guerrilla combatants. Here, there were intersecting dynamics. The murder of women was interpreted through a deeply sexist, patriarchal, and racial lens. Because of this distortion, often, there was no conviction, and if ever convictions occurred, they were of lighter sentences. At Independence, for instance, most women were murdered in what became known as the Gukurahundi (Shona for the early rain which washes away the chaff before the spring rains) or the Matabeleland Massacre. It has been estimated that 20,000 Ndebele people were murdered during this period. Since the constitutional referendum in 2000, Zimbabwe has had a history of controversial parliamentary and presidential elections characterized by systematic attacks on women. Both state and non-state political actors have used women as "weapons of war" to "punish or persecute the political party to which women belong." The killing is a method of instilling political fear, domination, and control, as the murder is predetermined therefore selective of the women killed.

State-sponsored femicide is also used to delegitimize opposition parties by pointing fingers at rivalries. Women are more targeted than men because it's easy to raise attention. New insights came from young women who reside in rural areas and are in opposition politics. They said they are specifically targeted with severe gendered forms of crime, including femicide. They suffer four layers of political injustices. Firstly, they suffer injustice because they are women in general. Secondly, injustice affects them as young women. Thirdly, violence affects them as young women in opposition politics. Fourthly, injustice affects them as young women in rural areas where avenues for recourse are next to none. For them approaching justice institutions such as police could lead to re-traumatization. Justice institutions deter them from seeking justice because of costs and cumbersome court procedures. Sometimes there are no apparent femicide differences between wartime and peacetime countries. Peacetime countries are not different from the early 1990s, where the armed conflict in Rwanda, Burundi, Liberia, and Sierra Leone, among others, had disproportionately targeted women to silence contending groups. The eventual murder is on the continuum of abduction, torture and sexual assault, decapitation, mutilation, and dumping of dead bodies in disused mines or dams, asphyxiation or strangulation, stabbing, beating, or shooting by firearm. Political institutions organically undermine women's free and fair participation in politics because politics is a preserve of those with the capacity to perpetrate violence. Men are political gatekeepers. They have the keys. Politics has become an unsafe venture for most women.

POTENTIAL INTERVENTIONS

There is a need to improve tactical training and specialization in the criminal justice system. It is imperative to subject police and magistrates to guidelines and analytical tools such as the eco-feminist model used to investigate femicides. In Zimbabwe, there is also a need for specific femicide legislation, including codifying the crime of femicide in the bill and publishing investigatory and adjudicatory manuals for femicide cases. This might also include creating the Minimum Guidelines for Investigation of Crimes Against Women and Femicide and the Manual to Judge with a Gender Perspective make protocols relevant for this investigation. Lessons can be drawn from South Africa, which has established the Gender-Based Violence Command Centre and an R1.6-billion Emergency Response Action Plan on Gender-Based Violence and Femicide to improve access to justice for women. South Africa is the only Southern African country establishing a femicide watch dashboard.

CONCLUSION AND FUTURE RESEARCH

Research shows that the killing of women in Zimbabwe manifests in varying degrees. Yet there hasn't been any rigorous and systematic research on the factors that precede such killings. The research evidence from the high prevalence of femicide indicates interesting directions for future research. First, there is a gap in understanding femicide. Literature on women and violence in Zimbabwe has advanced significantly for the past three decades. However, femicide continues to evade attention.

Zimbabwe is increasingly experiencing new typologies of femicide that have escaped policy and scholarly notice. For instance, women who are forced to commit suicide through torture and harassment fall outside the dominant understanding of femicide. There is a need to extend the scope of femicide definition by adopting the term "extended femicide." In the process of femicide research, interviewees revealed that women are increasingly participating in the murder of men. However, the factors motivating women's involvement in murder are not known. The effects of such participation also deserve more attention.

RECOMMENDED READINGS

Adèle, Kirsten. 2007. *Guns and Roses: Gender and Armed Violence in Africa*. Geneva: United Nations Development Programme.

Campbell, Jacquelyn, and Carol Runyan. 1998. "Femicide: Guest Editors' Introduction." *Homicide Studies* 2 (4):347–370. doi:10.1177/1088767998002004001.

Caputi, Jane, and Diana Russell. 1990. *Femicide: Speaking the Unspeakable*. New York: Harrington Park Press.

Claire, Laurent, Michael Platzer, and Maria Idomir. 2013. "Femicide: The Power of a Name." In *Femicide: A Global Issue That Demands Action*. Vienna: ACUNS.

Corradi, Consuelo, Chaime Marcuello-Servós, Santiago Boira, and Shalva Weil. 2016. "Theories of Femicide and Their Significance for Social Research." *Current Sociology* 64 (7):975–995. doi:10.1177/0011392115622256.

Cultural Atlas. 2022. "Zimbabwean Culture." http://culturalatlas.sbs.com.au/zimbabwean-culture/familya52a7f05-b70c-4dd0-ae5e-743faf142831.

Dawson, Myrna. 2016. "Punishing Femicide: Criminal Justice Responses to the Killing of Women over Four Decades." *Current Sociology* 64 (7):996–1016. doi:10.1177/0011392115611192.

Dobash, Emerson, and Dobash Russell. 2015. *When Men Murder Women*. Oxford: Oxford University Press.

Henrik, Belfrage, Susanne Strand, Jennifer Storey, Andrea Gibas, Randall Kropp, and Stephen Hart. 2012. "Assessment and Management of Risk for Intimate Partner Violence by Police Officers Using the Spousal Assault Risk Assessment Guide." *Law and Human Behaviour* 36 (2) 60–67. doi:10.1007/s10979-011-9278-0.

Iranzo, Juan Manuel. 2015. "Reflections on Femicide and Violence against Women." Working Paper on Femicide (Unpublished), GESES: Universidad de Zaragoza.

Jill, Radford, and Dianna Russell. 1992. *Femicide: The Politics of Woman Killing*. Buckingham: Open University Press.

Jiménez, Patricia, and Fernández Ana. 2017. *Feminicide: A Global Phenomenon from Brussels to San Salvador*. EU: Brussels.

Johansson, Fanny. 2021. *Femicide as a Form of Gender-Based Violence against Women in International Human Rights Law: Critique of Current Regulation and Suggestions for Future Development*. Orebro: Orebro Universitet.

Kambarami, Maureen. 2006. *Femininity, Sexuality and Culture: Patriarchy and Female Subordination in Zimbabwe*. South Africa: University of Fort Hare.

Keith, Thai, Hyslop Fran, and Richmond Robyn. 2022. *A Systematic Review of Interventions to Reduce Gender-Based Violence among Women and Girls in Sub-Saharan Africa. Trauma Violence Abuse*. California: Sage.

Lightfoot-Klein, Hanny. 1989. *Prisoners of Ritual: An Odyssey into Female Genital Mutilation in Africa*. New York: Harrington Park Press.

López, Geofredo Angulo. 2019. "Femicide and Gender Violence in Mexico. Elements for a Systematic Approach." *The Age of Human Rights Journal* (12):158–183. doi:10.17561/tahrj.n12.9.

Magdalena, Grzyb, Marceline Naudi, and Chaime Marcuello-Servós. 2018. In Shalva Weil, Consuelo Corradi and Marceline Naudi. *Femicide across Europe: Theory, Research and Prevention*. Bristol: Policy Press.

Marcuello-Servós, Chaime, Consuelo Corradi, Shalva Weil, and Santiago Boira. 2016. "Femicide: A Social Challenge." *Current Sociology* 64 (7):967–968. doi:10.1177/0011392116639358.

Marieke, Liem, and Frans Koenraadt. 2018. *Domestic Homicide: Patterns and Dynamics*. London: Routledge.

Medie, Peace. 2018. *The Police: Laws, Prosecutions, and Women's Rights in Liberia*. Cambridge: Cambridge University Press.

Medie, Peace. 2019. "Women and Violence in Africa – Online Publication."

Medie, Peace, and Kang Alice. 2018. "Power, Knowledge and the Politics of Gender in the Global South." *European Journal of Politics and Gender* 1 (1):37–54. doi:10.1332/251510818X15272520831157

Méndez, Crippa, and Rodríguez Barraza. 2022. "An Interpretation of Femicide in Mexico: Violence and Human Rights." *Advances in Applied Sociology* 12 (1):11–28.

Miguel, Edward. 2005. "Poverty and Witch Killing." *The Review of Economic Studies* 72 (4):1153–1172. doi:10.1111/0034-6527.00365.

Mukamana, Jeanette Iman'ishimwe, Machakanja Pamela, and Adjei Nicholas Kofi. 2020. "Trends in Prevalence and Correlates of Intimate Partner Violence against Women in Zimbabwe, 2005–2015." *BMC International Health and Human Rights* 20 (1):1163–1186.

Muluken, Muluneh, Stulz Virginia, Lyn Francis, and Kingsley Agho. 2020. "Gender-Based Violence against Women in Sub-Saharan Africa: A Systematic Review and Meta-Analysis of Cross-Sectional Studies." *International Journal of Environmental Research and Public Health* 17 (2):1–21.

Radford, Jill. 1992. "Introduction." in J. Radford and D. E. H. Russell (eds.), *Femicide: The Politcs of Woman Killing*, edited by J. Radford and D.E.H. Russell. New York: Twayne, pp 3–12.

Radford, Jill, and Diana E. H. Russell. 1992. *Femicide: The Politics of Woman Killing*. New York: Twayne.

Russell, Diana E. H. 2011. "The Origin and Importance of the Term Femicide," www.dianarussell.com/origin_of_femicide.html

Standish, Katerina. 2021. "Everyday Genocide: Femicide, Transicide and the Responsibility to Protect." *Journal of Aggression, Conflict & Peace Research*. doi:10.1108/JACPR-10-2021-0642.

Standish, Katerina, and Shalva Weil. 2021. "Gendered Pandemics: Suicide, Femicide and Covid-19." *Journal of Gender Studies* 30 (7):807–818. doi:10.1080/09589236.2021.1880883.

UN Women. 2021. *Global Database on Violence against Women*. Harare: UN Women Zimbabwe Chapter.

UNODC. 2018. "Global Study on Homicide." *United Nations Office on Drugs and Crime*. Vienna: Austria.

Weil, Shalva. 2016. "Making Femicide Visible." *Current Sociology* 64 (7):1124–1137. doi:10.1177/0011392115623602.

Weil, Shalva. 2020. "Gendering Coronavirus (Covid-19) and Femicide." *European Sociologist* 45 (1):1–4

Weil, Shalva, Consuelo Corradi, and Marceline Naudi. 2018. *Femicide across Europe: Theory, Research and Prevention*. Bristol: Policy Press.

Zengenene, Susanti. 2019. "Violence against Women and Girls in Harare." *Zimbabwe. Journal of International Women's Studies* 20 (9):18–36.

Femicide, Harmful Practices, Religious Organizations and the Law in the North Caucasus

SAIDA SIRAZHUDINOVA

This article shows the main results of the author's practical work as a sociologist and civil rights activist. The article analyzes the results of the first qualitative research on the problems of femicide, which is based on traditions and, thanks to this, finds support and approval among residents of the North Caucasus. In the article we will consider the main forms of femicide (honor killings, female genital mutilation, and reproductive violence). The article also analyzes how the authorities and religious organizations solve the problem of femicide.

INTRODUCTION

The North Caucasus is the common name of several republics with a dominant Muslim population, located on the southwestern borders of Russia. There are more than 4 million people live in the region. Muslims and the population is increasing due to the very high birth rate in the region. The North Caucasus is distinguished by the rapid growth of Islamization of both traditional "folk" Islam, in which religion and local traditions, pre-Islamic rituals are closely intertwined, and new Salafist trends for the region. The extremes of one direction and the other can be dangerous for women.

Femicide in the article refers to the murder of women as a result of domestic violence. The author places special emphasis on femicide based on the protection of the honor of the family. "Honor killings" is a vivid example of femicide that occurs in order to rehabilitate the honor of the family in the eyes of society. "Honor killings" and female genital mutilation traumatizing girls are associated with an attempt to prevent inappropriate behavior of women and harming the honor of the family.

Traditionalist femicide is psychological violence against women of the region (communities), through control over the sexuality of women, monitoring compliance with traditional norms attributed to women, punishing women for violating traditions. Femicide manifests itself in preventive actions (female genital mutilation, demonstrative punishments for violations of norms, intimidation, control, threats, reproductive violence) as well as direct physical murder of women (for example, honor killings).

All of the forms of femicide are currently common in the region. There are many forms of violence against women (World Health Organization 2012) as honor killings, genital mutilation (Rakić 2017), reproductive violence, forced abortions or forced pregnancy), emotional violence, psychological violence, financial violence, pressure and control in the region (Sirazhudinova 2017).

Femicide in North Caucasian society is associated with the traditional ideas of the local population about honor, sexual control and order in society.

They receive nourishment in the traditions and customs common in the minds of the people supporting harmful practices. In the Caucasus a woman's body and soul belong to the male members of her family (Sirazhudinova 2021, 58).

The support of femicide by the people is connected with the desire to resist globalization and transformations of society through control over women and femicide.

Currently, both men and women themselves approve of honor killing in order to sustain a family's reputation, so they consider it important to preserve their society and follow religion. Harmful practices in their view are associated with the requirements of Islam.

Femicide is justified by "the interests of the patriarchy"(McIntosh 1978), "the interests of honor" (Arin 2001) (Cetin 2015) and "suppression as subordination to the rules, which confirms one's belonging to a social group» (Fuko1996)".

In this paper the issues surrounding femicide as sexual control are considered from a feminist standpoint, together with the universality of human rights, and the reason why Caucasian society is dominated by sentiments associated with cultural relativism (Fluehr-Lobban 1995; Zechenter 1997).

METHODS

In 2021, I investigated the influence of traditions on femicide and harmful practices (honor killings and female genital mutilation in the republics of the North Caucasus). These problems were first voiced and investigated by human rights defenders in the period from 2016-2021. During this period, 4 human rights reports were published (Female

Genital Mutilation 2016), (Antonova 2018) which made a wide resonance in Russian society and caused a sharp debate. I studied the impact of reports and publications in the media on the problem of FGM and honor killing in the region, along with examples of the rejection of the practice in a number of regions of Dagestan and Chechnya.

Twenty-five interviews were conducted by author with women from both FGM practicing and previously FGM practicing regions within Dagestan and Chechnya and with experts. The interviews showed that publication of the reports of the Legal Initiative did not go unnoticed in society.

When analyzing the problem of honor killing as a traditional femicide, the author refers to the results of research (interviews) conducted in the republics of the North Caucasus on this issue from 2016-2021.

RESULTS AND DISCUSSION

Interviews conducted with women and experts from the North Caucasus confirmed the connection of traditional femicide with the problems of honor killings and female genital mutilation.

FGM is femicide because of this harmful practice as a human rights violation and a form of honor-based violence. FGM practice is not murder in the literal sense, but it poses a threat to women's lives, as it is carried out in unsanitary conditions and by unskilled specialists, but by ordinary, often illiterate women. This practice is aimed at killing women's sexuality, and entails wide-ranging negative impacts on girls' physical and mental health for life.

It is important to focus on these issues in this article. For a more vivid illustration of the peculiarities of justifying femicide by traditions and the difficulties of combating harmful practices, I give examples from the respondents' answers.

FEMALE GENITAL MUTILATION

My respondents noted that after the practice of female circumcision came to wider public attention, women from practicing areas began to discuss this issue on social networks (most notably WhatsApp). These women shared their experiences, with some commenting on the negative impact of the practice on their lives:

> "The practice has affected my life very much. The consequences are catastrophic for me. Because of the operation, I am experiencing real problems in the field of sexual relations ." (Interview with a woman from Dagestan. Makhachkala. Summer 2021).

I also found villages and districts that have abandoned the practice of FGM. Unfortunately, the examples of rejection of the practice in the post-Soviet period are rare. In general, the practice of FGM continues to exist in the republics of the North Caucasus, despite the publication of reports attracting wide public attention.

The process of abandoning the practice of FGM was not a simple one. On the one hand, the refusal was partially initiated by the community itself. One woman revealed that

> "The imam (Qadi Suleymanov) banned female circumcision, after men who were dissatisfied with the consequences of the practice addressed him. The men came to the imam (7-8 people) and complained about the woman who was performing female circumcisions. The imam called her to him and asked how she did it. She said that she cuts off more for the beautiful girls, not less, because husbands love beautiful women. Ugly women retain at least a vestige of the organ. The imam forbade her to perform these crippling operations. It stopped for a while. Then another woman began to circumcise the girls. The imam called her to the sofa (where the Sharia court is held) and asked about her activities. She replied that she hadn't been doing anything lately because there were a lot of complaints from the men. One told her "to make your hands wither", and "don't do this!" So the imam told all the women through his wife that no one would perform mutilation on the girls. After him, the men of the community also forbade their wives to take the girls away. The girls had previously been taken for this operation at the age of 3 (sometimes at the age of 5), and the women had been promised money for the operation on their children" (Interview with a woman from a village in the mountains of Dagestan. Gimry village. Spring 2021).

Some rural imams (especially those who studied in Syria) also forbid the practice of FGM, but they emphasize that

> "I can't jump over Muftiyat (the official Muslim religious organization of the republic). It is not necessary to advertise that I have forbidden, but we should not perform this crippling operation! Don't do this to the girls!" (Interview with a woman from a village in the mountains of Dagestan. Spring 2021 (The place is not specified, for the sake of preserving the anonymity of the imam)).

The imam who forbade female circumcision for girls also ridiculed the idea of the invalidity of Namaz (prayer) without circumcision.

On the other hand, in interviews respondents noted that society (especially women) tried to maintain the practice, despite the ban of the Qadi (judges in the Sharia Muslim court) and the statement about the undesirability of the procedure.

According to the study, of 25 women who went through the procedure of female circumcision, the majority then continued the practice on their children. Of these, only 4 women did not have their daughters circumcised. A major reason for this is movement to the plain. Most practicing villages are located far from cities, many mountaineers move to the plain in search of work and more comfortable living conditions. Migration to a large city diminishes the influence of the community on a person's life and his social circle expands accordingly. Despite the fact that the number of immigrants from the mountains to the plain, and those living in Georgia where the practice of FGM is preserved rose, there was no reduction in the number of advocates of the procedure because, as a rule, migrants settle into tight-knit communities and their collective interdependence and reliance upon tradition persists, regardless of the place of residence. Secondly, the rejection of the practice in a village in the Untsucul district for religious reasons was due to young Salafi theologians who were educated in Syria trying to establish Shi'at (based on the norms of Islam) control over society. A third reason was marrying a resident from a non-practicing area.

A survey of experts showed difficulties in discussing the problem of female circumcision in the North Caucasus. This meant that 78% of experts refused to be interviewed.

Most experts (principally doctors) recognized the existence of the practice and its horrific consequences.

> "This is a terrible problem. And it's bad for your health. The problem leads to septic infections, as well as to psychological trauma. In order for a woman not to fornicate, this was regulated by adat (a custom). A woman's clitoris is cut off so that she does not fornicate" (Interview with a man doctor from Kizilyurt (Dagestan). Summer 2015).

> "This is impractical and there is no justification for the operation. Everything that is given to a person, he needs, this is how he was created, conceived. But this is the custom of Adat and it is not possible to fight it by force. You need to explain and talk to people. It's not doctors who are needed here, it should be done by the Muftiat – the official religious organization. Because there is no religious justification for this (Interview with a men doctor from Mahachkala (Dagestan). Summer 2015).

"I heard that previously the clitoris was cut. Now most often a scratch is made with a sharp knife . It is believed that this deprives a woman of pleasure and thus restrains her. But now we seem to agree that there are many ways for a woman to have fun. It doesn't make sense, but the people live like this, and these are separate peoples. These are very specific peoples. " (Interview with a men doctor from Mahachkala (Dagestan). Summer 2015)

Many women living in rural areas in local communities strive to preserve the practice and inflict it on their daughters. This is illustrated by the example from the interview given above. We see that even after the ban on FGM by the imam, women still tried to have their daughters circumcised. An indicative response is that of a woman interviewed by us in the Dagestan mountains who stated

"These are our traditions. No one will forbid us to observe our traditions. We have always done female circumcision. So it's necessary. " (Interview with a woman from Dagestan. Tsuntinsky district. Summer 2020)

I was able to find only a few examples of rejection of the practice of FGM. Many of these were related to the efforts of religious figures banning the practice.

Given the role of religious figures in banning the practice together with the opinion of experts, this problem in the North Caucasus will not be solved in the near future. Here, the largest and most influential official religious organization, the Spiritual Administration of Dagestani Muslims, continues to promote the practice of FGM, calling on the residents of the republic to continue female circumcision through the Assalam newspaper (the material was removed after a wide public discussion). The fatwa (decision) issued by the local muftiate in August 2020 prohibits only extreme forms of female circumcision and approves the most common form in the region - type IV circumcision - cutting off all or part of the clitoris, as well as an incision or scratch on the clitoris for the purpose of blood-letting. The fatwa was a response to a film about female circumcision in Dagestan (This, 2020).

HONOR KILLING

Despite the fact that the term "honor killing" is absent from local terminology and adats (Adat is a local custom that regulates the life of the inhabitants of a particular community. Some adats are unwritten, and are transmitted orally. Some are fixed in customary law (the Code of Adats of individual societies), this problem, according to respondents, is connected with perceptions of family honor, with shame and stain (in the ordinary view) and with the "immoral behavior" of the victim, in court and in legal documents.

> "In Dagestan or Chechen languages, this term loses all meaning. We don't have such a concept. This is a different linguistic world. In normal times, we haven't heard of this for decades. Moreover, this topic remains taboo. It is not customary to discuss this in society or in the family circle. There is a taboo in society that is not talked about. This term is not recognized in Chechen. We didn't know what it was. Maybe this has happened, but decent Chechens will never discuss certain topics." (Interview with a man human rights defender. The Chechen Republic. June 2016.)

> "The honour of a woman is not only her honour, it is also the honour of the family. For example, in the Caucasus, we have one person, she is not separated from the world of everything. I would also not bring it to the court or to the law enforcement agencies. I will decide this issue within my family" (Interview with a man historian. The Chechen Republic. June 2016).

Even now many residents of the region are ready to justify "honor killings".

> "Honour killings are a huge deterrent. I am against murder, but the preservation of society is very important". (Interview with a man from NGO. The Chechen Republic. June 2016)

> "This is a demand for girls. Girls should always take care about honor. Girls are responsible for the honor of the family. It's not much. Our girls are used to always thinking about honor and to control the behavior, words and especially relationship with men" (Interview with a woman from NGO. The Chechen Republic. June 2020)

Consequently this abhorrent practice still finds adherents. Society as a whole is not ready to fight or condemn it. It is important to note that women are more critical in this matter. 78% of the women surveyed consider the practice to be barbaric while only 32% of men oppose the practice. "Honor killing" finds great support among the residents of Chechnya and Ingushetia. This is despite the fact that history and adats show that honor killings were never a local custom.

Women view "honor killings" more condemningly. Women who have lost their loved ones and survived the tragedy due to harmful practices are especially critical.

> "This is an unfair tradition. Girls are often slandered. Very often, enemies, in order to hurt the family, start up false gossip. Girls are killed to wash away the stain and "whitewash the face of the family." That's how girls become innocent victims." (Interview with a woman whose niece was murdered. The Chechen Republic. June 2020)

Women have noted an increase in threats to women's lives recently. Men seduce or rape women, and then blackmail women, extort money from them, threaten to damage their honor more and more often. There are more such cases every year. Threats to women's lives are also increasing.

CONCLUSIONS

Femicide in the North Caucasus is currently increasing. People are increasingly trying to follow neo-traditions and ideas about religion promoted by religious authorities. Therefore, the term traditional femicide was used in the work. Since femicide feeds here and thrives thanks to the traditions in the region. Harmful practices are currently finding supporters. Those people who are aware of the harm from traditions that carry violence against women are not ready to speak openly and are silent, fearing the condemnation of the majority. It is dangerous to talk about issues such as honor killings in Chechnya and Russia. A vivid example of this is the surveillance of an activist and the author of reports on honor killings in the North Caucasus (Legal Initiative 2018). An activist, Elena Chufelina, who is engaged in helping victims of domestic violence (Gender 2019), was attacked, and a fabricated criminal case was brought before her.

Femicide in Russia is very difficult to stop, because the state policy is aimed at maintaining patriarchal order. Women's problems are usually ignored. Local religious Muslim organizations either support harmful practices (the position of the Spiritual Administration of Muslims of Dagestan on female circumcision), or ignore these problems and remain silent.

Therefore, the main recommendation is to conduct educational work with the population, consolidate civil society in demanding the adoption of laws protecting women and prohibiting harmful practices. Given the situation in the country, it can be assumed that if the state recognizes the problem, then religious organizations will also be forced to oppose practices that have been banned by many authoritative Muslim theologians and that create negative stereotypes.

FUNDING

Russian Science Foundation (RSF) № 22-28-00484, https://rscf.ru/en/project/22-28-00484/

ORCID

Saida Sirazhudinova http://orcid.org/0000-0002-6069-6076

RECOMMENDED READINGS

Antonova, YuA, and S. V. Sirazhudinova. 2018. Killed by gossip "Honor killings" of women in the North Caucasus. Report on the results of a qualitative study in the republics of Dagestan, Ingushetia and Chechnya (Russian Federation). https://www.srji.org/upload/medialibrary/a3d/PPI-2018-12-18-Honor-killings-Eng-final.pdf.

Arin, C. 2001. "Femicide in the Name of Honor in Turkey." *Violence against Women* 7 (7):821–825. doi:10.1177/10778010122182758.

Cetin, I. 2015. "Defining Recent Femicide in Modern Turkey: Revolt Killing." *Journal of International Women's Studies* 16 (2):346–360.

Female Genital Mutilation of Girls in Dagestan (Russian Federation). 2016. https://www.srji.org/upload/iblock/52c/fgm_dagestan_2016_eng_final_edited_2017.pdf

Fluehr-Lobban, C. 1995. "Cultural Relativism and Universal Rights." *The Chronicle of Higher Education* 1–2:B.

Fuko, M. 1996. *Volia k Istine: Po tu Storonu Znaniia, Vlasti i Seksual'nosti: Raboty Raznykh Let [the Will to Truth: Beyond Knowledge, Power and Sexuality: Works of Different Years]*. Moscow: Kastal.

Gender problems and domestic violence in the Rostov region [online]. 2019. http://center-kmu.ru/bez-rubriki/gendernye-problemy-i-domashnee-nasilie-v-rostovskoj-oblasti

"Legal Initiative" receives threats after "honour killings" report. 2018. https://www.eng.kavkaz-uzel.eu/articles/45475/

McIntosh, M. 1978. "Who Needs Prostitutes? The Ideology of Male Sexual Needs," in C. Smart and B. Swart (eds.), *Women, Sexuality and Social Control*, 53–64. London: Routledge & Kegan Paul.

Rakić, J. 2017. "Female Genital Mutilation-from Tradition to Femicide." *Temida* 20 (2): 241–267.

Sirazhudinova, S. 2017. "I Can't Tell about It": the Domestic and Sexual Violence in the Republics of the North Caucasus (Based on the Sociological Research Data in the Republic of Dagestan)." *Woman in Russian Society* 4 (4) :26–35. doi:10.21064/WinRS.2017.4.3.

Sirazhudinova, Saida. 2021. "The Women Organizations and Activism in Combating Domestic Violence in the North Caucasus." *Journal of International Women's Studies* 22 (11) :57–63. https://vc.bridgew.edu/jiws/vol22/iss11/6.

This is happening here. 2020. https://www.youtube.com/watch?v=Gu-PAHqfMUY

World Health Organization. 2012. *Understanding and Addressing Violence against Women: femicide (No. WHO/RHR/12.38)*. Geneva: World Health Organization.

Zechenter, E. 1997. "In the Name of Culture: cultural Relativism and the Abuse of the Individual." *Journal of Anthropological Research* 53 (3) :319–347. doi:10.1086/jar.53.3.3630957.

Africa's Code of Honor and the Protection of Women

Komlan Agbedahin

INTRODUCTION

Although domestic and international legal instruments have played a central role in the protection of women against femicide in wartime and peacetime in Africa, a recourse to values embedded in African philosophies could play a catalytic role in this humanistic mission. Accordingly, this essay proposes that African values should hold more significance in the fight for the protection of women.

Violence against women is a global phenomenon. *The Forgotten Casualties of War: Girls in armed conflicts*, the title of a report of Save the Children (2005) captures the horrendous experiences of girls and young women in war-torn countries in Africa. There is evidence that even in African countries without war, women are frequently forgotten casualties of gender-based violence. According to the United Nations Under-Secretary-General and UN Women Executive Director, this social malady is "an epidemic in all societies, without exception" and every day "on average, 137 women are killed by a member of their own family" (Mlambo-Ngcuka 2020). Although the 2017 homicide victim global statistics show that 80% of victims are men and 20% women, "of the totality of intimate partner homicide, 82% of the victims were women, and 18% men" (Sparknews 2021). The *Global Study on Homicide 2018* of the United Nations Office on Drugs and Crime (UNODC) revealed the complex nature of this crime which involves both men and women as perpetrators:

> even though men are the principal victims of homicide globally, women continue to bear the heaviest burden of lethal victimization as a result of gender stereotypes and inequality. Many of the victims of 'femicide' are killed by their current and former partners, but they are also killed by fathers, brothers, mothers, sisters and other family

members because of their role and status as women. (United Nations Office on Drugs and Crime (UNODC) 2018, 11)

According to global statistics on domestic violence killings of women and girls, "Africa is the region in which women run the greatest risk of being killed by their intimate partner or family members" (Sparknews 2021). Although the aim of this essay is not to establish the existence of this phenomenon in Africa, it is worth mentioning a few cases. In South Africa, once called the "Rape Capital of the World," gender-based violence characterized by rape and femicide, is a reality (Gqola 2016; Adebayo 2019; Brodie 2020); the gruesome killing of women during "Women's Month" confirms the devastation and overwhelming nature of this social ill (Magaisa 2021; SANews.gov.za 2021). Women are also being murdered in the Democratic Republic of Congo (DRC), according to the United Nations Joint Human Right Office, where shockingly, the government armed forces that are tasked to protect civilians against armed groups are also perpetrators. Recent killings in the North Kivu and Ituri provinces attest to this ("293 civilians were killed in August 2021, including 63 women and 24 children") (United Nations 2021). In Tanzania, older women accused of witchcraft are often attacked (Van Steenbergen 2012). Witch-hunt killings and other forms of femicide also take place in DRC (Mossi and Duarte 2006; Agence France-Presse in Bukavu 2021). Nigeria is also affected by the violence against women. According to Amnesty International's report on Nigeria:

> On a daily basis, women are beaten and ill-treated for supposed transgressions, raped and even murdered by members of their family. In some cases, vicious acid attacks leave them with horrific disfigurements. Such violence is too frequently excused and tolerated in communities and not denounced. Husbands, partners and fathers are responsible for most of the violence against women. (Abayomi and Kolawole 2013, 55)

The magnitude of the multifaceted femicide phenomenon affecting Africa is indicative of a deep crisis of protection for women in times of both war and peace. Besides domestic laws, there are international legal instruments including the Vienna Declaration and World Conference on Human Rights; the Declaration of the Elimination of Violence Against Women, adopted by the UN General Assembly in 1993; the Convention on the Elimination of All Forms of Discrimination Against Women (CEDAW) 1979; the Universal Declaration on Human Rights 1945; the Platform for Action from the United Nations fourth World Conference on Women held in Beijing (Abayomi and Kolawole 2013) to ensure the protection of women against violence. The question this paradox raises is why the steady increase in this phenomenon despite the existing protection mechanisms. The answer to this question is the crux of this essay: there is too little emphasis on the role African philosophies (upon which communities hinge) could play in the protection of women. This negligence allows for a "crafty labelling" of international and even domestic laws meant to protect women as alien and oppressive legal instruments by perpetrators. I argue that, to a great extent, strands of African philosophies are embedded in many international instruments, and the onus is on specific African countries to tease out these values and ensure ownership by Africans. The dissonance between the political ownership and cultural ownership of protection instruments needs to be addressed; it is important to ensure a shift from the rhetoric of "government laws" to "our laws."

FEMICIDE AS A GLOBAL SCOURGE

There is a growing body of literature on femicide (Arin 2001; Mathews, Jewkes, and Abrahams 2015; Weil 2016; Cullen et al. 2019; García-Del Moral 2018; Bouzerdan and Whitten-Woodring 2018; Brodie 2020; McPhedran et al. 2018; Musila 2021). Although this phenomenon has been diversely examined by scholars across disciplines, in this essay, the focus is on recent relevant works, especially those revolving around the magnitude and visibility of femicide, and methodological challenges associated with studying femicide, as well as the legal protection conundrum, mischaracterization, and possible solutions. In her book *Femicide in South Africa,* Brodie (2020) considered contradictory and paradoxical narratives and misinformation which characterize the description and interpretation of this phenomenon. This suggests the need for a phenomenological approach to understanding femicide because of the richness of individual experiences. As Brodie (2020, 1) pointed out, "individual stories matter, a lot, because when women die, they are not and should never be considered as just statistics". Superficial analyses make femicide invisible. This invisibility was brought to the fore earlier by Weil (2016) in her article *Making femicide visible.*

With reference to South Africa, "intimate femicide, the killing of a woman by an intimate partner, is the leading cause of female murder" (Mathews, Jewkes, and Abrahams 2015, 107). This is facilitated by an assertion of power and control related to masculinity. Musila (2021, 17) described the corrosive nature of femicide by pointing out that "toxic heteropatriarchy" has transformed the country into "a femicidal graveyard littered with women's broken bodies and maimed spirits." Mathews, Jewkes, and Abrahams (2015, 107) recommended that "the gendered context" be taken into consideration when planning and implementing interventions.

The study of femicide is not without methodological challenges and weaknesses (Corradi et al. 2016; Cullen et al. 2019; McPhedran et al. 2018). Using intimate partner femicide (IPF) as an example, McPhedran et al. (2018) pinpointed methodological challenges related to the study of femicide. They argued that victim-focused methodological approaches such as "analysing official data sources", "interviewing proxies of the victim", "treating near-lethal violence as an analogue for lethal violence", "a synthesis approach: combining data sources" (McPhedran et al. 2018, 62-63) have limitations which impede robust debates about femicide. Accordingly, McPhedran et al. have suggested the psychological autopsy (PA) for the study of femicide.

> PA combines extensive quantitative and qualitative data gathered from in-depth interviews with proxies of the deceased … with data from official records. It captures – in a structured and systematic way – unique, detailed, and critical individual information (including, for example, life history, psychosocial factors, and help-seeking behaviours) that is not generally collected in official records. …. However, researchers have not yet taken advantage of full PA methodology to study IPF victimisation. This represents a fruitful direction for future consideration. (McPhedran et al. 2018, 64)

Similarly, Corradi et al. (2016) proposed a theoretical and methodological mixture for more fruitful scholarship on femicide and advanced a multidisciplinary approach for the study of femicide. In their article *Counting Dead Women in Australia: An In-Depth Case Review of Femicide*, Cullen et al. (2019, 1) recommended that "future research should target identification of risk and protective factors, and improved coordination of data collection".

Other recent works on femicide contribute to the evolvement of this phenomenon and key underpinning theories. Suggested theoretical pathways comprise the feminist approach, the sociological approach, the criminological approach, human rights approach and the decolonial approach (Corradi et al. 2016, 9). According to Corradi et al. (2016, 9), femicide is "a complex social phenomenon". This complexity was echoed by Paulina García-Del Moral (2018) in her study *The Murders of Indigenous Women in Canada as Feminicides: Toward a Decolonial Intersectional Reconceptualization of Femicide*. Drawing on "a decolonial intersectional framework", she argued that "it is necessary to go beyond a radical feminist definition of femicide to analyze the murders of Indigenous women as racialized gendered violence". Factors such as "power inequalities" and the "politics of exclusion" are crucial for the reconceptualization and analysis of femicide (García-Del Moral 2018, 949). This complexity points to the need for multifarious strategies to tackle this social malady.

In Turkey, the number of women killed by "their relatives, spouses or significant others" (Muftuler-Bac and Muftuler 2021, 159) is on the increase. One key factor which accounts for this state of affairs is the "provocation defence" which

> ... allows Turkish men to receive lenient sentences when they commit femicide, i.e. murder their wives, girlfriends, female relatives, or partners ... Provocation defence in gender-based violence rests on claims that women's initial actions violate societal norms and traditions. ... Femicide is an integral part of the male dominance as part and parcel of this social structure. Social norms, cultural mores, traditions and values all add up to be utilized in judges' rulings on femicides. ... The Court decisions – Criminal Courts and Court of Cassation – are used to reproduce and sustain male domination over women. (Muftuler-Bac and Muftuler 2021, 160–170)

Shared complicities allowing for femicide are evident in the Turkish case which epitomizes social values and norms used for evil purposes. Whether femicide in the name of honor (Arin 2001) or intimate femicide (Mathews, Jewkes, and Abrahams 2015, 107), femicide stems from gendered power differentials embedded in social norms and values (Hudson as cited in Bouzerdan and Whitten-Woodring 2018). The aforementioned Turkish situation is a case in point, whereby societal norms and values are used for self-annihilation. This essay counters the Turkish example, by showing how African philosophies, norms, and values, centered on human dignity, could contribute to lessening the scourge of femicide if properly channeled. The essay shows that Ubuntu and the Africa's Code of Honor, rather than having corrosive effects on society, values and recognizes the worth and preciousness of human lives, particularly the lives of women. These values contain adequate antidotes to femicide.

HUMAN DIGNITY, AFRICA'S CODE OF HONOR, UBUNTU – AN ANTIDOTE TO FEMICIDE IN AFRICA?

I argue that the protection of women and human beings in general will remain a mirage if it is not centered on human dignity. This protection should be viewed as a humanization project based on human dignity. This concept has been topical in political, cultural, philosophical, human rights, activism, social and economic rights, as well as human relations discourses (Egonsson 1998; Chan and Bowpitt 2005; Benhabib 2011; Bonefeld and Psychopedis 2005; Heyman 2008; Carey, Gibney, and Poe 2010; Lindner 2011; Kateb 2014; Agbedahin 2020). We need to go beyond initial debates which tend to equate human dignity with "honor linked to social status, position, social order, social recognition" (Hobbes 1996, as cited in Bonefeld and Psychopedis 2005, 4). Some scholars suggest that dignity should be separated from "position and social status" (Bayefsky 2013, 810). Krause (2002, 15), for instance, argued that all human beings are entitled to "the intrinsic worth of a human being". Accordingly, the onus is on people to ensure that dignity is reciprocal; being givers and receivers of dignity should be a guiding principle of our relationship with other human beings regardless of race, gender, class, nationality or any categories. Women are no exception. Kant put this into perspective by observing that, "human beings have 'an intrinsic worth' or 'dignity' that makes them valuable 'above all price'" (Rachels 2012, 136). Accordingly, they should be treated "as ends in themselves" and not "mere means" (Bognetti, as cited in Bayefsky 2013, 811). Kateb (2014, 6) supported this view asserting: "I cannot claim just for myself or my group but must claim for all human beings". The onus is on human beings regardless of their social status, class, or race, to ensure that other human beings are treated equally with dignity.

In Africa, the respect for this human dignity is premised on core values or philosophies. I argue that the erosion of these values has paved the way for the ubiquitous and immoral protection crisis, particularly the protection of women in Africa. For the purpose of further discussion in this essay, the focus will be on Africa's Code of Honor and Ubuntu both of which embody human dignity.

Yolande Diallo's (1976) research on the comparison of African traditions and humanitarian law, focused on human dignity. She described how, in pre-colonial Africa, women and children were protected during wars, contra the predatory nature of contemporary armed conflicts in Africa. For instance, in Niger "women and children who remained in the village were protected by a group of warriors … To attack a village where there are only women and children is not war; it is theft" (Diallo 1976, 9). Women were also peacemakers: "In Togo, it is interesting to note, when men were preparing for war, the women used to leave the village shouting: 'Do not fight, we are all brothers' or 'If you kill someone, you kill him for yourself'" (Diallo 1976, 9). Diallo (1976, 16) further pointed out that "fighting was subject to a genuine code of conduct. For instance, it was forbidden to kill women, children or old people; to strike an enemy from behind; to profane certain places or to kill a disarmed enemy." This approach to war during the pre-colonial era was guided by Africa's "Code of Honour."

In his address delivered at the 2001 Public Annual Lecture of the National Association of Political Science Students (NAPSS), at the University of Ibadan, Nwolise (2001, 1) pointed out that women "constitute the sacred sources of life". Paradoxically, these precious sources of life are not properly protected. He put this into perspective by referring to the fate of the vulnerable in armed conflict situations in Africa. He pointed out how the treatment of women, children and the aged symbolizes an erosion of the values upon which African society hinges:

> the present barbaric, savage, and bestial attacks, inhuman and undeserved treatment women, children and the aged are subjected to in contemporary Africa's (violent) conflict theatres and situations constitute a serious threat to the survival, continuity and development of the Black race and African people and must be checked now. ... I insist with all sense of humility, that as Africans, we have lost our bearing, and gone astray, far away from our social values and path of honour; and e need to retrace our footsteps now. (Nwolise 2001, 4)

Nwolise (2001) argued that the redemptive pathway which could end such inhuman treatment of women involves the imperative return to Africa's Code of Honor, a traditional code "based squarely on the social values of the people" (Nwolise 2001, 12). He argued that the Code

> refers to a set of moral principles accepted by a society for ensuring good personal character, justice, equity and fairness in interpersonal and intergroup relations, inculcating a strong sense of what is morally right in order to produce people of honour, good behaviour, truthfulness, and great reputation. This code is often stronger than law as people are honour bound to do certain things even when the law does not require them to do so. ... it is like an oath and a solemn promise. ... When Africa's Code of Honour is mentioned, I refer to that corpus of generally accepted principles guiding, regulating, and propelling individual and group attitude, action and behaviour in all spheres of human interaction, along the path of moral uprightness, honour, good personal character, truth, justice, equity, fairness, humanness, trust, confidence, and Godliness. This code was not written but it existed, and when people deviated from or violated it, they were sanctioned accordingly. It was expressed in proverbs, and idioms, and practised as part of the customs and traditions of different African societies on whose social values the Code was based. (Nwolise 2001, 6-7)

Some of the values underpinning Africa's Code of Honor and which are germane to the protection of women are linked to African social values including the sacredness of human life and sanctity of human blood; the inviolability of the family; the marriage institution; women as the sacred sources of life; children as blessings from God, hope of the family, insurance against old age, and source of lineage and group continuity; good family and personal name; proper training and upbringing of children to be useful, responsible and good members of society; good health, progress, and long life; good neighborliness; being one's brother's keeper; property and wealth honestly acquired; living a moral life – immorality did not only bring loss of face, but also spiritual defilement and the wrath of God; justice, equity and fairness (especially in sharing public or private resources); accommodation, tolerance, and compromise; high degree of value placed by Africans on human life and blood; protection of human life (Nwolise 2001, 12-14).

Nwolise (2001, 17), referring to the protection of women during wars pointed out that "women, children, the aged, and visitors were never attacked in war. They were protected. Women were never molested or assaulted". Using Senegal and Niger as examples, he indicated that "during wars, women, children, and the aged were removed to the sea if it was perceived that war will reach villages or towns. In areas of today's Niger, women and children were protected in villages by warriors, and to attack a village where women and children were kept was regarded as an act of cowardice and theft, not war "(Nwolise 2001). He stressed that the

> inviolability of women, children, and the aged was one of the most cherished rules in the conduct of war in all parts of Africa. …Women were regarded, protected, and respected as the sacred sources of life necessary for regenerating the society and ensuring its survival and continuity, apart from their other contributions to societal development. Thus, they were immune from attack during periods of war. (Nwolise 2001, 19)

In order to return to or redeem Africa's Code of Honor, Nwolise (2001, 30-31) suggested "a clear programme of cultural revival without minding complaints from foreign religious groups who were part of the original conspiracy against African culture, social values, and code of honor". He further indicated that the revival of the Code of Honor should be done through mainstream education, and "through the media, churches and mosques, handbills and pamphlets to purge off the diseased social values already existing in the minds of Africans from the times of slavery, colonialism, and military rule" (Nwolise 2001, 31). While Nwolise's (2001) approach to the cultural revival may seem radical, it could be moderated through Ubuntu, as the ultimate goal of this cultural revival (at the least within the scope of this essay) is to ensure the protection of women in Africa.

The African philosophy of Ubuntu, diversely described, hinges on the belief that other human beings are an extension of a particular human being, thus indicative of an invariable connectedness between human beings. This suggests that any human being who lives without other human beings is not a human being – "being human through others" according to Mugumbate and Nyanguru (2013, 82). Badian's (1972, 27) assertion that "a human being is nothing without other human beings. He/she comes into the world through their hands and leaves the world through their hands" (author's translation) epitomizes this philosophy. Ubuntu can also be described as "a social contract through which other people are given proper respect and dignity" (Agbedahin 2021). According to Archbishop Desmond Tutu, Ubuntu connotes "the essence of being human, and it is part of the gift that Africa will give the world … I am human because I belong. It speaks about wholeness. It speaks about compassion" (Tutu as cited in Hailey 2008, 2-3). The direct translation from Zulu of Ubuntu is "I am because of who we all are" implying a sense of self through others. It is based on humanism and is "a social and humanistic ethic". One key dimension of Ubuntu can be considered germane to the protection of women:

> to be human is to affirm one's humanity by recognizing the humanity of others and, on that basis, establish respectful human relations with them; second, if and when one is faced with a decisive choice between wealth and the preservation of the life of another human being, then one should opt for the preservation of life (Samkange and Samkange cited in Mugumbate and Nyanguru 2013, 84).

From the aforementioned analyses and explanations, Ubuntu revolves around sympathy, benevolence, solidarity, hospitality, generosity, sharing, openness, kindness, caring, harmony, interdependence, obedience, collectivity consensus life, dignity, care, compassion, humaneness, and reconciliation. In other words, "people who espouse ubuntu fight to produce good lives and to elaborate social conditions for lives to be lived well" (Chasi 2021, 8). According to Chasi (2021,18), "it is particularly important that ubuntu is not presented in overly simplistic and optimistic terms". Chasi (2021) also highlights the value of the concept of the warrior:

> … the warrior, in metaphoric terms, reveals and situates the human capacity to act with agency that breaks down barriers, climbs over mountains, and worms through problems. The figure of the warrior expresses the capacity of people to secure survival by means of abilities to fight, destroy, and protect." (4)

I argue that in order to confront the scourge of femicide, Africans need to embrace this warrior aspect of Ubuntu. If through Ubuntu, people could remember that African culture hinges on humanity and humanness, harmony, dignity, compassion and reciprocity, and embrace others with the belief and sense that "your pain is my pain, my wealth is your wealth, your salvation is my salvation" (Nussbaum 2003, 21), profound protection of women would become a reality.

CONCLUSION

In this essay, I have highlighted that femicide is a reality in contemporary Africa. I have also demonstrated that contra the pre-colonial era when the protection of women particularly during wars was based on Africa's Code of Honor, the protection of women in contemporary Africa is based on international legal instruments namely conventions, principles, agreements and declarations. I have argued that contrary to perceptions of these international legal instruments as purely foreign legal tools, these protection instruments to a certain degree embody African values which have been underemphasized. I therefore argue that to ensure the protection of women, African values within these instruments should be highlighted. This will allow for a more inclusive protection approach devoid of political and economic suspicions. It would also allow for a shift from the longstanding perception of both domestic and international legal instruments for protection as 'oppressive state laws' to 'our protection instruments'. People need to understand that international legal instruments for protection are not alien or colonial tools or strategies to control or vilify them but can be viewed as modernized forms of African protection values which existed in pre-colonial times as observed by Diallo (1976). 'Africa's Code of Honor' and 'Ubuntu' are vehicles of these redemptive values and their revivification could contribute enormously to the protection of African women against femicide.

The revivification of these value is not meant to antagonize existing legal protection instruments but rather to establish how the latter can be seen as an extension of Africa's Code of Honor. These legal instruments can be seen as also originating from Africa and not as being totally imposed by the West. It is important to negotiate ownership. There is need for revival of Africa's Code of Honor to strengthen international and domestic initiatives for the protection of women in Africa. It is an issue of acceptability rather than substitution to achieve protection goals. As Diallo pointed out

> many principles expressed in the Geneva Conventions are to be found in the law of war in pre-colonial Africa. It was only after the introduction of slavery and the inroads of colonialism into Africa south of the Sahara that traditional societies began to disintegrate,

causing the code of honour to fall into disuse in war. However, the memory of this code of honour is kept alive in the narratives of the storytellers, and the code perhaps could be revived as a means of humanizing present-day conflicts. (Diallo 1976, 16)

Africa's Code of honor and Ubuntu teach human beings to see other human beings as extensions of themselves. Although the revivification of African values is not a panacea for the violence against women in Africa, it holds promise if intentionally, methodically, and ethically done. A femicide-free Africa is possible.

ACKNOWLEDGEMENTS

I would like to thank Rhodes University for appointing me as Research Associate in the Department of Sociology.

ORCID

Komlan Agbedahin http://orcid.org/0000-0001-5715-1879

RECOMMENDED READINGS

Abayomi, A. A., and T. O. Kolawole. 2013. "Domestic Violence and Death: Women as Endangered Gender in Nigeria." *American Journal of Sociological Research* 3 (3): 53–60.

Adebayo, B. 2019. "A Post Office Worker was Given Three Life Sentences for Raping and Murdering a Student. Now South African Women Are Saying Enough." *CNN*, November 15. https://edition.cnn.com/2019/11/15/africa/south-africa-student-murder-sentence/index.html

Agbedahin, K. 2020. "Crisis of Human Dignity and Mega Sporting Events Tragedies," in J. Kocián, J. Mlynár, and P. Hoffmannová, *Malach Center for Visual History on Its 10th Anniversary: Compendium of Papers of the Prague Visual History and Digital Humanities Conference 2020*, 119–132. Prague: MatfyzPress.

Agbedahin, K. 2021. "'Covid-Preneurship' and the Imperative Return to Ubuntu." *Peace Review* 33 (1): 80–87. doi:10.1080/10402659.2021.1956133.

Agence France-Presse in Bukavu. 2021. *Witch-hunt murders surge in Democratic Republic of Congo*. September 28. https://www.theguardian.com/world/2021/sep/28/witch-hunt-murders-surge-democratic-republic-congo-women-south-kivu-province

Arin, C. 2001. "Femicide in the Name of Honor in Turkey." *Violence against Women* 7 (7): 821–825. doi:10.1177/10778010122182758.

Badian, S. 1972. *Sous L'orage (Kany) Suivi de la Mort de Chaka*. Paris: Presence Africaine.

Bayefsky, R. 2013. "Dignity, Honour, and Human Rights: Kant's Perspective." *Political Theory* 41 (6): 809–837. doi:10.1177/0090591713499762.

Benhabib, S. 2011. *Dignity in Adversity: Human Rights in Troubled Times*. Cambridge: Polity.

Bonefeld, W., and K. Psychopedis. 2005. *Human Dignity*. Burlington: Ashgate.

Bouzerdan, C., and J. Whitten-Woodring. 2018. "Killings in Context: An Analysis of the News Framing of Femicide." *Human Rights Review* 19 (2): 211–228. doi:10.1007/s12142-018-0497-3.

Brodie, N. 2020. *Femicide in South Africa*. Cape Town: Kwela Books.
Carey, S., M. Gibney, and S. Poe. 2010. *The Politics of Human Rights*. New York: Cambridge University Press.
Chan, C. K., and G. Bowpitt. 2005. *Human Dignity and Welfare Systems*. Bristol: Policy Press.
Chasi, C. 2021. *Ubuntu for Warriors*. Trenton: Africa World Press.
Corradi, C., C. Marcuello-Servos, S. Boira, and S. Weil. 2016. "Theories of Femicide and Their Significance for Social Research." *Current Sociology* 64 (7): 975–995.
Cullen, P., G. Vaughan, Z. Li, J. Price, D. Yu, and E. Sullivan. 2019. "Counting Dead Women in Australia: An in-Depth Case Review of Femicide." *Journal of Family Violence* 34 (1): 1–8. doi:10.1007/s10896-018-9963-6.
Diallo, Y. 1976. *African Traditions and Humanitarian Law: Similarities and Differences*. Geneva: International Committee of the Red Cross.
Egonsson, D. 1998. *Dimensions of Dignity: The Moral Importance of Being Human*. Lund: Springer.
García-Del Moral, P. 2018. "The Murders of Indigenous Women in Canada as Feminicides: Toward a Decolonial Intersectional Reconceptualization of Femicide." *Signs: Journal of Women in Culture and Society* 43 (4): 929–954. doi:10.1086/696692.
Gqola, P. D. 2016. *Rape: A South African Nightmare*. Johannesburg: Jacana Media.
Hailey, J. 2008. *Ubuntu: A Literature Review*. London: Tutu Foundation.
Heyman, S. J. 2008. *Free Speech and Human Dignity*. New Haven, CT: Yale University Press.
Kateb, G. 2014. *Human Dignity*. Cambridge, MA: Belknap Press.
Krause, S. R. 2002. *Liberalism with Honor*. Cambridge, MA: Harvard University Press.
Lindner, E. G. 2011. *A Dignity Economy*. Lake Oswego: Dignity Press.
Magaisa, T. 2021. "The Killing Doesn't Stop During South Africa's Women's Month." *Human Rights Watch*, August 30. https://www.hrw.org/news/2021/08/30/killing-doesnt-stop-during-south-africas-womens-month
Mathews, S., R. Jewkes, and N. Abrahams. 2015. "'So Now I'm the Man': Intimate Partner Femicide and Its Interconnections with Expressions of Masculinities in South Africa." *British Journal of Criminology* 55 (1): 107–124. doi:10.1093/bjc/azu076.
McPhedran, S., L. Eriksson, P. Mazerolle, and H. Johnson. 2018. "Victim-Focussed Studies of Intimate Partner Femicide: A Critique of Methodological Challenges and Limitations in Current Research." *Aggression and Violent Behavior* 39: 61–66. doi:10.1016/j.avb.2018.02.005.
Mlambo-Ngcuka, P. 2020. *COVID-19: Women Front and Centre* (Statement by Phumzile Mlambo-Ngcuka, UN Under-Secretary-General and UN Women Executive Director). *unwomen.org*, March 20. https://www.unwomen.org/en/news/stories/2020/3/statement-ed-phumzile-covid-19-women-front-and-centre
Mossi, M., and M. Duarte. 2006. *Violence against Women in the Democratic Republic of Congo (DRC)/Alternative Report Prepared for the Committee on the Elimination of Discrimination against Women*. Geneva: World Organisation Against Torture. https://reliefweb.int/sites/reliefweb.int/files/resources/A3DE086259F013EC492571CC00114EE7-omct-cod-15aug.pdf.
Muftuler-Bac, M., and C. Muftuler. 2021. "Provocation Defence for Femicide in Turkey: The Interplay of Legal Argumentation and Societal Norms." *European Journal of Women's Studies* 28 (2): 159–174. doi:10.1177/1350506820916772.
Mugumbate, J., and A. Nyanguru. 2013. "Exploring African Philosophy: The Value of Ubuntu in Social Work." *African Journal of Social Work* 3 (1): 82–100.
Musila, G. A. 2021. "Yearning for Rootedness in a Femicidal Landscape." *Safundi* 22 (1): 15–18. doi:10.1080/17533171.2020.1823740.

Nussbaum, B. 2003. "Ubuntu: Reflections of a South African on Our Common Humanity." *Reflections: The SoL Journal* 4 (4): 21–26. doi:10.1162/152417303322004175.

Nwolise, O. 2001. *The Fate of Women, Children and the Aged in Contemporary Africa's Conflict Theatres: The Urgent Need to Revive Africa's Code of Honour*. Lecture delivered at the 2001 Public Annual Lecture of the National Association of Political Science Students (NAPSS), University of Ibadan Chapter, at the Lady Bank Anthony Hall, University of Ibadan on Wednesday, August 15, 2001. Ibadan, Oyo, Nigeria: Department of Political Science, University of Ibadan.

Rachels, S. 2012. *The Elements of Moral Philosophy*. 7th ed. New York: McGraw-Hill.

SANews.gov.za. 2021. "Nzimande Conveys Condolences to Mtebeni Family." *SAnews.gov.za*, August 23. https://www.sanews.gov.za/south-africa/nzimande-conveys-condolences-mtebeni-family

Save the Children. 2005. *The Forgotten Casualties of War: Girls in Armed Conflicts*. London: Save the Children. https://resourcecentre.savethechildren.net/pdf/2717.pdf

Sparknews. 2021. "Facts and Figures: Global Domestic Violence Numbers." *Mail & Guardian*, June 22. https://mg.co.za/news/2021-06-22-facts-and-figures-global-domestic-violence-numbers/

United Nations Office on Drugs and Crime (UNODC). 2018. *Global Study on Homicide 2018*. Vienna: United Nations Office on Drugs and Crime. https://www.unodc.org/documents/data-and-analysis/GSH2018/GSH18_Gender-related_killing_of_women_and_girls.pdf.

United Nations. 2021. "Summary Killings, Human-Rights Abuses Surge in Eastern DRC." *Aljazeera*, September 29. https://www.aljazeera.com/news/2021/9/29/summary-killings-human-rights-abuses-surge-eastern-drc

Van Steenbergen, M. 2012. "Witchcraft Used as Excuse for Violence Against Older Women in Tanzania." *The Guardian.com*, October 1. https://www.theguardian.com/global-development/2012/oct/01/witchcraft-violence-older-women-tanzania

Weil, S. 2016. "Making Femicide Visible." *Current Sociology* 64 (7): 1124–1137. doi:10.1177/0011392115623602.

Femicide Prevention Strategy Development Process: The South African Experience

NWABISA SHAI ⓘ, LEANE RAMSOOMAR ⓘ AND NAEEMAH ABRAHAMS ⓘ

Despite surveys to measure the magnitude of femicide, civil action to garner public recognition and, government commitment to respond effectively to femicide, South Africa lacked a comprehensive strategy to inform femicide prevention. This essay outlines the process South Africa followed to develop a femicide-specific prevention strategy and argues for an evidence and practice informed approach in a context where femicide prevention is limited. The strategy for South Africa was developed using a phased, research-driven and consultative approach over six months. Its development was informed by expert review of a previous draft strategy, key multi-sectoral stakeholder consultations and literature on femicide, leading to an evidence-based socio-ecological model of the drivers of femicide and a robust theory of change. A country-level definition of femicide was developed. Subsequently, five (5) key strategic objectives were prioritized: strengthening of legislation and policy; leadership and accountability; building evidence and practice informed femicide prevention; and institutional strengthening. However, successful implementation of the femicide prevention strategy is underpinned by reliance on evidence, practice and contextual relevance; urgency to develop and test prevention innovations; intergovernmental collaboration to ensure effective case management from investigation to sentencing; and political leadership to address challenges and conflicts pertaining to government performance targets and policies.

INTRODUCTION

Femicide is the most extreme form of Gender-Based Violence (GBV) globally. Global studies have shown about a third (30-38.6%) of women are

---

This is an Open Access article distributed under the terms of the Creative Commons Attribution-NonCommercial-NoDerivatives License (http://creativecommons.org/licenses/by-nc-nd/4.0/), which permits non-commercial re-use, distribution, and reproduction in any medium, provided the original work is properly cited, and is not altered, transformed, or built upon in any way.

killed by an intimate partner (Stöckl et al. 2013; United Nations Office on Drugs and Crime 2018). The proportion of women killed by a partner is six times higher than the proportion of murdered men killed by a partner (38·6% and 6·3% of female and male homicides (Stöckl et al. 2013). While GBV has been recognized as a social and public health problem disproportionately affecting women based on their gender by the UN Committee on the Elimination of Discrimination Against Women (CEDAW) at its Eleventh Session in 1992[1], only in 2013 did the UN General Assembly (UNGA) adopted a resolution to act against femicide (gender-related killings) under resolution 68/191[2]. However, the term "femicide" was first mentioned by Diana Russell nearly half a century ago in 1976 and many years of limited research and action followed until the period just before the 2013 UNGA resolution (Campbell and Runyan 1998; McFarlane et al. 1999; Dobash, Dobash, and Cavanagh 2009; Campbell et al. 2003; Sharps et al. 2001). This was followed by a significant growth in research with increased understanding of the extent of femicide across many settings. This included clarification of terminology, its drivers, prevention, and policy development through multi-sectoral collaborations, namely the four year 'Femicide across Europe' project (Weil, Corradi, and Naudi 2018; Campbell et al. 2003, 2007a, 2007b; Dobash, Dobash, and Cavanagh 2009; Stöckl et al. 2020; Weil 2016). Similar advances have also been observed in Latin America (García-Del Moral 2016; Fragoso 2013; Bravo 2008). While definitional contestations continue (Neumann 2022; Russell 2012; Weil 2016; Weil, Corradi, and Naudi 2018), documentation and monitoring of femicide has grown incrementally over the past decade particularly through death reviews, femicide censuses, observatories, and femicide watches recommended by the UN Special Rapporteur on violence against women, Dubravka Šimonović (Dawson 2017; Cullen et al. 2019; Long et al. 2020; Šimonović 2016). Although understanding the extent of the problem is the first step in prevention and a route to awareness raising and advocacy, there should be concerted effort and policy on how to prevent femicide which is distinguished from GBV prevention.

South Africa faces an epidemic of structural and direct violence (IPV and non-partner sexual violence) (Machisa et al. 2011; National Department of Health (NDoH) et al. 2019; Gass et al. 2011; Jewkes et al. 2011), and gross income and gender inequalities for a country almost 30 years its post-

---

[1]Gender-based violence was defined by the U.N. Convention for the Elimination of All Forms of Discrimination against Women (1992) as "violence that is directed against a woman because she is a woman, or violence that affects women disproportionately. It includes acts that inflict physical, mental or sexual harm or suffering, threats of such acts, coercion and other deprivations of liberty" (General Recommendation No. 19).

[2]United Nations Resolution 68/191, on 'Taking action against gender-related killing of women and girls', fn. 1., adopted by the General Assembly at its 70th plenary meeting on 18 December 2013.

apartheid dispensation. It is also one of the few countries with a documented history of femicide research. The first national femicide survey showed a woman (aged 14 years+) was killed by an intimate partner every 6 hours in 1999. The second survey conducted in 2009 showed a significant decrease of femicide over the 10 years: 12.9 per 100 000 female population in 2009 compared to 24.7 per 100 000 in 1999 (Abrahams et al. 2012, 2013a). Despite the overall decrease, the proportion of intimate partner femicide amongst the cases where perpetrators were identified increased from 50.3% in 1999 to 57.1% in 2009. This meant that South Africa's intimate partner femicide rate in 2009 was almost 5 times higher than the global rate (5.6/100 000 compared to 1.3/100 000 female population in 2017 (United Nations Office on Drugs and Crime 2018; Abrahams et al. 2013a). A study on media coverage of femicide in South Africa during 2012/2013 found that media reports were not representative of femicide in the country: less than 20% of femicides were reported in the media, femicide was inaccurately constructed, namely, more coverage of certain victims (elderly and white victims), more reports of non-intimate partner femicide vs intimate partner femicide; and an over-emphasis of crime with higher newsworthiness (Brodie 2021). This study highlighted the important role of media as the primary source of information on femicide for many South Africans, how it influencing audiences and misrepresents reality of who should be feared as a perpetrator, and who is at risk of becoming a victim of femicide (Brodie 2019; Brodie 2021).

Surveillance of femicide should essentially become part of Government's monitoring of GBV in response to the Sustainable Development Goals (SDGs) (Goal 5: Target 5.2). However, poor systems and integration of data have prevented this to date. A Femicide Watch has been initiated, which aims to collate police data with the justice sector data but is not yet functional.

In 2018, South African civil society activists catapulted femicide into public recognition as a serious problem facing South African society, through a campaign that demanded government's commitment to recognizing femicide as a type of GBV that required a concerted effort for prevention and response. The campaign led to South Africa's first ever National Strategic Plan on Gender Based Violence and Femicide (NSP-GBVF) which was launched in April 2020 (Department of Women, Youth and Persons with Disabilities 2020), which emphasizes the use of an evidence-based GBV prevention and response approach. Prior to the finalization of the national strategy, an Emergency Response Action Plan (ERAP) with a 6-month target for implementation, highlighted critical gaps in legislation, case management for rape and femicide and protection orders among others (Government of South Africa 2020). Moreover, the Department of Justice and Constitutional Development (DOJ&CD) were already in the process of developing a prevention strategy for femicide prior to the civil action leading to the NSP-GBVF. The femicide strategy development process was halted to contribute toward the shared government and civil society GBVF prevention and response agenda. Upon review of the national strategy however, policymakers noted that the NSP-GBVF lacked articulation of femicide as a distinct GBV form, that requires a unique approach for prevention. This essay outlines the process of developing a femicide-specific prevention strategy for South Africa and makes an argument for an evidence and practice informed approach in a context where femicide prevention is limited.

THE PROCESS OF DEVELOPING THE NATIONAL INTEGRATED STRATEGY ON THE PREVENTION OF FEMICIDE

The DOJ&CD commissioned the authors who are GBV and Femicide researchers to develop a femicide prevention strategy that would be integrated with the NSP-GBVF and ERAP documents. The expected outcomes included a clear definition and understanding of femicide, drivers of victimization and perpetration, guidance for GBVF policymakers, practitioners and other allied stakeholders on prevention measures, programmes and services, and advice on the strengthening of the information and data management systems.

Over a 6-month period, authors developed the femicide prevention strategy following a phased, research driven approach. This involved expert review of the previous draft femicide prevention strategy by key multi-sectoral stakeholders and structures working on GBVF namely, civil society organizations, academics, policymakers, and development partners applied a femicide lens to the document. Next, a desktop review of national and international literature on femicide was conducted and informed the development of an evidence and practice informed socio-ecological framework to understand the drivers of femicide victimization and perpetration in the South African context. A femicide-specific lens was applied to the development of a Theory of Change (ToC) for femicide prevention. The ToC outlines the problem statement, from which flows a set of hypothesized barriers to femicide prevention, and a set of inputs and activities required to achieve measurable outcomes and impact.

A Country-Level Definition of Femicide

It emerged during key stakeholder consultations that an agreed country-level definition of femicide was a critical first step in the strategy

> **The agreed country-level definition of femicide:**
> *Femicide is the killing of a female person regardless of the person's age, gender identity, or sexual orientation, whether committed directly or indirectly by another person.*

Figure 1. Country-level definition of femicide for South Africa.

development (Figure 1). This was developed by a multi-disciplinary working group of legal, social, and judicial experts through a series of workshops, and accounted for global and local contexts and experiences. The country-level definition was further divided into two main types: intimate partner and non-intimate partner femicide (Figure 2).

The working group agreed that the South African definition should be inclusive of all forms of femicide, should be operationalized for administrative, monitoring, and research purposes and not for legal purposes. The group recognized that femicide was already part of South African legislation (Criminal and Related Matters Amendment Bill) which criminalizes murder, a violation of the most fundamental human right – that of the right to life, as enshrined in the South African Bill of Rights (Government, South Africa 1996; Campbell, Webster, and Glass 2009), thus not warranting allocation as a separate crime category in this first phase of the strategy.

Several key considerations were made during the definition development process. The working group envisaged this femicide definition would enable data collection from the current South African administration data systems, namely female killings reported by the South African Police Services (SAPS), for continuous monitoring of femicide as part of the key outcomes identified in the NSP-GBVF, and by specialized systems such as the Femicide Watch, which can provide information on subtypes of femicides. The definition also includes female killings of all ages, as intimate relations commonly start early (Gupta and Mahy 2003; Richter et al. 2015), and child death reviews and surveys show increasing levels of sexual femicide of younger children (Abrahams et al. 2017). Further, the working group acknowledged that forcing femicide into a single category can be problematic as multiple subtypes of femicide exist in South Africa and globally. For example, a transgender person could be

> *The two main types femicide defined as:*
>
> *•Intimate partner femicide: the killing perpetrated by a current or previous intimate partner, whether they are of the same or opposite gender, and where intimate relationships include marriage according to any law, custom, or religion; dating or customary relationship; live or lived together in a relationship like marriage; are or were engaged; proposal for intimate relationship was rejected; are or were in an actual or perceived romantic relationships; or any other intimate or sexual relationship of any duration.*
>
> *•Non-intimate partner femicide: the killing perpetrated by a person other than an intimate partner including a stranger, family member, relative or any acquaintance.*

Figure 2. The two main types of femicide: intimate partner femicide and non-intimate partner femicide.

killed and raped by a stranger and this femicide can fit into three types of femicide: non-intimate partner femicide, femicide of a transgender person, and sexual femicide.

Evidence Informed Socio-Ecological Model for Femicide Drivers in South Africa

To understand drivers of femicide we adapted a socio-ecological model which described femicide drivers, as with IPV, at multiple levels, i.e., individual, relationship, community, and societal levels (Bronfenbrenner 1979). We did not identify a femicide-specific model and adapted a country-specific model reflecting drivers of femicide in the South African context. The literature review confirmed the limited knowledge on risk factors for femicide, particularly non-intimate partner femicide, and reflected the low priority and state of knowledge accorded to femicide globally. Combining our own knowledge, those from other South African experts, and the local and global literature, we built an understanding of risk factors for femicide in South Africa (Campbell et al. 2003, 2007b; Weil, Corradi, and Naudi 2018; Boira, Tomas-Aragones, and Rivera

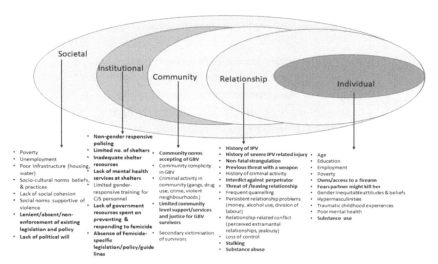

Figure 3. Socio-ecological model of femicide developed for South Africa.

2017; Gould 2015; Mathews, Jewkes, and Abrahams 2015; Dobash, Dobash, and Cavanagh 2009; Stöckl et al. 2020; Adinkrah 2014).

Inequitable gender and social norms that accept, normalize and are even complicit with violence were common threads across the multiple levels. We extended our model by adding the institutional level, as many identified drivers made this a critical addition, such as the lack of a risk or danger assessment tool and safety plans for femicide. Yet global literature highlights the risk and danger assessments and safety plans for femicide as key femicide prevention approaches although they intervene at the individual and relationship levels (Monckton Smith 2020). In the proposed socio-ecological model, we concur with the global perspective that it is a cluster of risk factors and not individual risk factors that increase risk for femicide. The adapted socio-ecological model provided a useful approach for both identifying multi-level drivers of femicide, and planning prevention efforts at these different levels (Figure 3).

A Synopsis of the Theory of Change for the National Integrated Femicide Prevention Strategy of South Africa

We developed a theory of change for femicide prevention based on global and national evidence, our engagement with key GBVF stakeholders, and our knowledge of the national context over more than two decades. While we found limited evidence on risk factors for femicide, we drew on the existing information to develop a series of theorized pathways from known country-specific and recognized drivers of femicide to, existing barriers to prevention, and developed a set of inputs and activities that would be required to achieve measurable outcomes and impact at multi-stakeholder levels. We considered five (5) key strategic objectives that needed to be implemented by all GBVF stakeholders at multiple levels that would result in the desired impact of fewer women, girls & gender diverse persons being killed in South Africa. A comprehensive version of the ToC is available in the strategic document, but for this paper we have outlined a truncated version (see Table 1). The main assumptions driving the effectiveness of this femicide strategy rests on a whole-of-society approach, optimal and robust implementation the NSP- GBVF with all efforts of policymakers, practitioners and funders based on femicide-specific evidence and practice.

Proposed Key Strategic Objectives for the National Femicide Prevention Strategy

We proposed five (5) key strategic objectives for the National Femicide Prevention strategy aligned to the priorities highlighted in the ERAP and NSP-GBVF documents. We considered these objectives to be the most realistic, implementable, and achievable at multi-sectoral levels within a short to medium term (2-5 years). Each activity was developed with indicators, time frames, and allocation of lead government departments and collaborators to ensure the strategy is effectively operationalized. These are listed below, (see also Table 2). To highlight a few, we acknowledged the need to review and develop femicide-prevention policy and guidelines and ensure their efficient and effective enforcement (see Key Strategic Objective 1). This should be accompanied by strong advocacy to ensure implementation and political leadership at the highest government level for commitment, accountability and resource prioritization (see Key Strategic Objective 2). The ToC acknowledged the lack of a surveillance system to monitor and evaluate femicide cases from police, mortuaries, and court data (see Key Strategic Objective 3). We further propose the implementation of a targeted, context-specific femicide prevention programme that will advance the research agenda for femicide prevention in South Africa (see Key Strategic Objective 4). This will focus on adapting two existing tools: risk assessment and safety plans for IPV, for femicide and testing its feasibility, acceptability and validity, and a longer term programme of research to evaluate what works to prevention femicide. Lastly, we emphasize the need to establish a dedicated and specialized femicide-specific unit led by the South African Police Service for

Table 1. Truncated theory of change for femicide prevention - South Africa.

	Fewer women, girls and gender non-conforming persons in South Africa die from femicide	
Impact		ASSUMPTIONS
Outcomes	<ul><li>Measurable progress in building evidence base on what works to prevent femicide in South Africa</li><li>Measurable evidence of effectiveness of femicide prevention and response interventions at multiple levels</li><li>Healthier and more positive relationships between couples</li><li>Dominant community norms changed to protect women, girls, and gender non-conforming persons from femicide</li><li>Strengthened individual and institutional capacity to effectively prevent and respond to femicide</li><li>Sustained political will to end femicide in South Africa, with adequate resources</li></ul>	<ul><li>Evidence-based policy and practice is needed to prevent femicide</li><li>Decision-makers use research evidence to inform their decision making</li><li>There is a conducive national framework for inter-sectoral collaboration to prevent and respond to femicide</li><li>Strengthening individual, community and institutional capacity will result in a reduction in femicide</li><li>All sectors recognize the need to address structural factors (poverty, unemployment etc.) as foundational in preventing femicide</li><li>Robust implementation of the NSP-GBV strategic objectives</li></ul>
Outputs	<ul><li>Increased number of women, girls and gender non-conforming persons recognizing femicide risk and linked to support services</li><li>Increased availability and use of substance abuse programmes</li><li>Decreased fire-arm related femicides in relationships</li><li>Increased availability and/or implementation of effective couples' programmes</li><li>Increased community practices promoting and modeling nonviolent and gender-equitable norms</li><li>A suite of evidence-based interventions to effectively prevent and response to femicide</li><li>Institutionalized national femicide surveillance system</li><li>Increased political will, and state resources for optimal prevention and response to femicide across all sectors</li><li>A suite of aligned legislation, policies, and guidelines to prevent and respond to femicide in South Africa</li></ul>	
Inputs	<ul><li>Prioritized multi-sectoral research programme on what works to prevent and respond to femicide</li><li>Optimal implementation of National Prevention Strategy on Gender-Based Violence and Femicide</li></ul>	

(Continued)

Table 1. (*Continued*).

	Fewer women, girls and gender non-conforming persons in South Africa die from femicide	ASSUMPTIONS
Impact	• Adaptation, development or scale up of couples' programmes • Better gun control as per the Firearms Control Act (FCA) • Sustained community-level norms change programmes that support survivors of violence in preventing femicide • Implement national surveillance program to measure magnitude and types of femicide • Building political will civil society and media advocacy for femicide prevention across all sectors	
Barriers	• Limited understanding of what works to prevent and effectively respond to femicide • Gun ownership • Substance abuse • Lack of awareness of danger signs for femicide (e.g., non-fatal strangulation) • Community norms accepting of GBV • Absence of femicide-specific policies and guidelines • Lack of political will to prioritize femicide prevention at global, national, and local government levels	
Problem statement	Femicide is the most extreme and severe form of GBV globally and is highly prevalent in South Africa. Most perpetrators of femicide are not convicted and incarcerated. Despite national efforts to address GBV through civil, legislative, and financial resources, femicide-specific prevention and response strategies remain extremely limited. There is a lack of consensus on definitions of femicide and limited surveillance, evidence-based femicide prevention programming and specialized technical training for femicide response personnel. Poor enforcement of existing legislation, and the absence of femicide-specific policy and guidelines, including the absence of specialized division for the management and investigation of femicides in SAPS, undermine efforts to effectively prevent and respond to femicide nationally and eliminate impunity for perpetrators.	

Table 2. Key strategic objectives for the national femicide prevention strategy.

KEY INTERVENTION	KEY ACTIVITIES	INDICATORS	TARGET*
STRATEGIC OBJECTIVE ONE: STRENGTHEN LEGISLATION AND DEVELOP FEMICIDE- SPECIFIC POLICY AND GUIDELINES TO PREVENT AND RESPOND TO FEMICIDE			
Review and enforce femicide prevention policy nationally	• Review, and develop femicide-prevention national policy framework with implementation plans	• Femicide-specific policy framework developed	Short-Medium term
	• Review, enforce and monitor existing legislation to ensure that it is responsive to femicide prevention	• Expedite Firearms Control Amendment Bill • Review the Maintenance Act 99 of 1998 • Enforce and monitor Criminal and Related Matters Amendment Bill (B17-2020), (2020); Domestic Violence Amendment Bill (B20-2020), and Criminal Law (Sexual Offenses and Related Matters) Amendment Bill, (2020) • Relevant legislation such as legislation related to marriage and marriage registrations, and any other.	Short-Medium term
STRATEGIC OBJECTIVE TWO: PROVIDE LEADERSHIP AND ACCOUNTABILITY FOR FEMICIDE PREVENTION			
Provide political leadership, dedicated resources and accountability through sustainable, multi-sectoral collaboration and action to prevent and respond to femicide	• Provide political oversight on implementation of the Femicide prevention strategy • Incorporate leadership of femicide prevention strategy into current GBVF national leadership structure (National GBVF Council)	• Adoption of femicide prevention strategy into relevant departmental Annual Performance Plans (APPs) by IMC-GBVF by target date* • Femicide prevention strategy is adopted by NSP-GBVF leadership structure (National GBVF Council)	Short-term

(Continued)

Table 2. (Continued).

KEY INTERVENTION	KEY ACTIVITIES	INDICATORS	TARGET*
	• Develop a costed plan of action for the implementation of the National Femicide Prevention Strategy	• Evidence for a budget allocated for all actions matching relevant department and their APPs	Short-term
	• Dedicate financial resources for the implementation and monitoring of the National Femicide Prevention Strategy through public-private funding partnerships (PPP)	• Evidence of dedicated budget allocation for femicide prevention	Short-term
STRATEGIC OBJECTIVE THREE: PRIORITIZE FEMICIDE SURVEILLANCE AND BUILD KNOWLEDGE OF WHAT WORKS TO PREVENT FEMICIDE			
Prioritization of the Development and Co-ordination of an integrated Information System to monitor femicide in SA	• Set up surveillance system using integrated administrative data from relevant departments (Femicide Watch)	• Femicide integrated information system developed, and surveillance reporting done on number and types of femicide by province per month	Short-term
	• Set up a rapid response tracking mechanism to track and monitor femicide cases using unique identifiers from police reporting through to the end of criminal justice system (Femicide Watch feeding into the IJS Transversal Hub)	• Femicide cases tracked through the police and justice system	Short-term
STRATEGIC OBJECTIVE FOUR: IMPLEMENT A TARGETED, CONTEXT-SPECIFIC FEMICIDE PREVENTION PROGRAMME			
Prioritize the implementation of a targeted, context specific femicide prevention intervention, and monitor and evaluate its effectiveness	• Prioritize and implement a research agenda on what works to prevent femicide	• Research agenda developed, and priority research funded	Short-Medium term
	• Review the current IPV risk assessment tool and safety plan for	• Tools reviewed, adapted and SOPs developed for use of tools with relevant institutions	

femicide prevention and adapt it for SA context drawing on global best practice		
Implement the adapted risk assessment tool and safety plan for femicide prevention as an emergency measure within the sectors	Evidence of implementation of contextualized risk assessment and safety plan tools for femicide prevention Evidence of rollout of risk assessment and safety plan tools nationally	Short-Medium term
Implement a femicide-specific public awareness raising campaign	Femicide-specific public awareness raising campaign developed and piloted as part of 365 days campaign Public campaigns implemented and monitored nationally (365 days campaign)	Short-term

STRATEGIC OBJECTIVE FIVE: STRENGTHEN INSTITUTIONAL CAPACITY TO PREVENT FEMICIDE

Strengthen the Criminal Justice System to deliver effective and efficient services to survivors of GBV and families of femicide victims, in alignment with Pillar 3: Protection, Safety, and Justice	Provide specialized training to the CJS on gender-responsive and femicide-specific guidelines	Training manual/s developed or adapted Modular training implemented with 100% of new entries of police, court personnel, magistrates, judges trained	Medium-term
	Set up a dedicated and specialized femicide-specific unit for management, investigation, prosecution and sentencing of femicide cases	A dedicated and specialized femicide-specific unit is set up, with ear-marked financial, human, and infrastructural resources	Medium-term

*Short term = 2022–2024: medium term = 2025–2026.

management, investigation, prosecution & sentencing of femicide cases (see Key Strategic Objective 5).

DISCUSSION

A South African femicide prevention strategy is a critical step toward building sustainable solutions to stem the epidemic of violence in a country with extreme rates of femicide. To develop the femicide prevention strategy, the authors had limited evidence from which to draw, though it is possible that femicide prevention strategies exist in other countries which are not publicly available. We critically appraised literature and distinguished femicide prevention from that of other forms of GBV and relied on evidence, practice, and contextual relevance. This was particularly important, as there is a dearth of data on the risk factors for femicide in the country and globally. Previous research (Prinsloo et al. 2017; Abrahams, Jewkes, and Mathews 2010; Abrahams et al. 2009, 2013b; Gould 2015; Mathews, Jewkes, and Abrahams 2011, 2015) provided a good basis for understanding factors influencing femicide victimization and perpetration across the ecological model. Our consultation with key stakeholders provided insights into critical aspects of policies and practice that enabled the identification of what was working well or not.

We also identified that the DOJ&CD had developed a risk assessment tool and safety plan for IPV, but very little is known about its uptake and impact. Given that the global evidence suggests that the use of 'danger' assessment tools implemented alongside safety plans can avert the escalation of IPV to femicide (Campbell, Webster, and Glass 2009), the authors saw this as an opportunity to adapt the existing IPV risk assessment tool and safety plan *for* femicide prevention and testing its effectiveness locally. This is one of the key strategic objectives that can be implemented within the short to medium term of the new femicide prevention strategy.

Many challenges in the implementation of the strategy are expected. A key intervention is the setting up of a dedicated unit to prioritize femicide cases that can ensure expert investigation and prosecution of perpetrators, which will also strengthen the much-needed surveillance system to link cases. Such a unit will require intergovernmental collaboration but may be challenged by conflicting priorities, performance targets and policies of government departments. Identifying the ideal structure to account for the implementation of the femicide strategy is another challenge. The South African government's Inter-Ministerial Committee on Gender

Based Violence and Femicide (IMC-GBVF) is the ideal structure in line with its role of facilitating political action, commitment, and resources.

The COVID-19 pandemic has further worsened the structural and gender inequalities globally (Ahinkorah et al. 2021; Casale and Posel 2020; Dekel and Abrahams 2021) and women's vulnerability to violence warrants urgent action. Femicide tracking and prevention remain a priority during the COVID-19 pandemic (Šimonović 2020). A five-year plan is an appropriate timeframe within which to prioritize action on femicide prevention because it aligns with government's Medium Term Strategic Framework (MTSF) approach and strategic intent to implement the National Development Plan (NSP) Vision 2030. The key strategic objectives build on existing legislation, services, and programmes, are achievable within the said timeframe, and can be planned for, resourced, and monitored by the IMC-GBVF. Multi-structural cooperation between the IMC-GBVF, National Planning Commission and Department of Planning, Monitoring and Evaluation are also required to ensure alignment of departmental priorities and performance targets and fast-track the implementation, monitoring, and evaluation of the new femicide prevention strategy.

FUNDING

This work was supported by South African Government - DOJ&CD; South African Medical Research Council.

ORCID

Nwabisa Shai http://orcid.org/0000-0003-4171-9129
Leane Ramsoomar http://orcid.org/0000-0003-1934-579X
Naeemah Abrahams http://orcid.org/0000-0002-6138-6256

RECOMMENDED READINGS

Abrahams, Naeemah, Rachel Jewkes, Lorna J. Martin, Shanaaz Mathews, Lisa Vetten, and Carl Lombard. 2009. "Mortality of Women from Intimate Partner Violence in South Africa: A National Epidemiological Study." *Violence and Victims* 24 (4):546–556. doi: 10.1891/0886-6708.24.4.546.

Abrahams, Naeemah, Rachel Jewkes, and Shanaaz Mathews. 2010. "Guns and Gender-Based Violence in South Africa." *South African Medical Journal = Suid-Afrikaanse Tydskrif Vir Geneeskunde* 100 (9):586–588. doi:10.7196/samj.3904.

Abrahams, Naeemah, Shanaaz Mathews, Rachel Jewkes, Lorna J. Martin, and Carl Lombard. 2012. "Every Eight Hours: Intimate Femicide in South Africa 10 Years Later." *South African Medical Research Council Research Brief* 2012:1–4.

Abrahams, Naeemah, Shanaaz Mathews, Carl Lombard, Lorna J. Martin, and Rachel Jewkes. 2017. "Sexual Homicides in South Africa: A National Cross-Sectional

Epidemiological Study of Adult Women and Children." *PLoS One* 12 (10):e0186432. doi:10.1371/journal.pone.0186432.

Abrahams, Naeemah, Shanaaz Mathews, Lorna J. Martin, Carl Lombard, and Rachel Jewkes. 2013a. "Intimate Partner Femicide in South Africa in 1999 and 2009." *PLoS Medicine* 10 (4):e1001412. doi:10.1371/journal.pmed.1001412.

Abrahams, Naeemah, Shanaaz Mathews, Lorna J. Martin, Carl Lombard, and Rachel Jewkes. 2013b. "Intimate Partner Femicide in South Africa in 1999 and 2009." *PLoS Medicine* 10 (4):e1001412 doi:10.1371/journal.pmed.1001412.

Adinkrah, Mensah. 2014. "Intimate Partner femicide-suicides in Ghana: Victims, offenders, and incident characteristics." *Violence against Women* 20 (9):1078–1096. doi:10.1177/1077801214549637.

Ahinkorah, Bright Opoku, John Elvis Hagan, Jr, Edward Kwabena Ameyaw, Abdul-Aziz Seidu, and Thomas Schack. 2021. "COVID-19 Pandemic Worsening Gender Inequalities for Women and Girls in Sub-Saharan Africa." *Frontiers in Global Women's Health* 2:686984. doi:10.3389/fgwh.2021.686984.

Boira, Santiago, Lucia Tomas-Aragones, and Nury Rivera. 2017. "Intimate Partner Violence and Femicide in Ecuador." *Qualitative Sociology Review* 13 (3):30–47. doi:10.18778/1733-8077.13.3.03.

Bravo, Soledad Rojas. 2008. "Femicide in Chilea." In *Strengthening Understanding of Femicide*. Washington, D.C.: PATH, Inter-American Alliance for the Prevention of Gender-based Violence (InterCambios), USAID, South African Medical Research Council, World Health Organization (WHO).

Brodie, Nechama. 2021. "Ideal Victims and Familiar Strangers: Non-Intimate Femicide in South African News Media." *African Journalism Studies* 42 (3):82–18. doi:10.1080/23743670.2021.1933559.

Brodie, Nechama R. 2019. "Using Mixed-Method Approaches to Provide New Insights into Media Coverage of Femicide." Doctoral diss., University of the Witwatersrand, Faculty of Humanities.

Bronfenbrenner, Urie. 1979. *The Ecology of Human Development: Experiments by Nature and Design*. Cambridge: Harvard University Press.

Campbell, Jacquelyn C., Daniel Webster, Jane Koziol-McLain, Carolyn Block, Doris Campbell, Mary Ann Curry, Faye Gary, et al. 2003. "Risk Factors for Femicide in Abusive Relationships: Results from a Multisite Case Control Study." *American Journal of Public Health* 93 (7):1089–1097. doi:10.2105/AJPH.93.7.1089.

Campbell, Jacquelyn C., Daniel W. Webster, and Nancy Glass. 2009. "The Danger Assessment: Validation of a Lethality Risk Assessment Instrument for Intimate Partner Femicide." *Journal of Interpersonal Violence* 24 (4):653–674. doi:10.1177/0886260508317180.

Campbell, Jacquelyn C., Nancy Glass, Phyllis W. Sharps, Kathryn Laughon, and Tina Bloom. 2007a. "Intimate Partner Homicide: Review and Implications of Research and Policy." *Trauma, Violence & Abuse* 8 (3):246–269. doi:10.1177/1524838007303505.

Campbell, Jacquelyn C., Daniel Webster, Jane Koziol-McLain, Carolyn Block, Doris Campbell, Mary Ann Curry, Faye Gary, Nancy Glass, Judith McFarlane, and Carolyn Sachs. 2007b. "Risk Factors for Femicide in Abusive Relationships: Results from a Multisite Case Control Study," in Mangai Natarajany (ed.), *Domestic Violence*, 135–143. London: Routledge.

Campbell, Jacquelyn, and Carol W. Runyan. 1998. "Femicide: Guest Editors' Introduction." *Homicide Studies* 2 (4):347–352. doi:10.1177/1088767998002004001.

Casale, Daniela, and Dorrit Posel. 2020. "Gender and the Early Effects of the COVID-19 Crisis in the Paid and Unpaid Economies in South Africa." NIDS-CRAM Policy Paper. Recuperado el, 18. Johannesburg: University of the Witwatersrand.

Cullen, Patricia, Geraldine Vaughan, Zhuoyang Li, Jenna Price, Denis Yu, and Elizabeth Sullivan. 2019. "Counting Dead Women in Australia: An in-Depth Case Review of Femicide." *Journal of Family Violence* 34 (1):1–8. doi:10.1007/s10896-018-9963-6.

Dawson, Myrna. 2017. *Domestic Homicides and Death Reviews: An International Perspective*. London: Palgrave Macmillan.

Dekel, Bianca, and Naeemah Abrahams. 2021. "'I Will Rather be Killed by Corona Than by Him…': Experiences of Abused Women Seeking Shelter during South Africa's COVID-19 Lockdown." *PLoS One* 16 (10):e0259275. doi:10.1371/journal.pone.0259275.

Department of Women, Youth and Persons with Disabilities. 2020. "National Strategic Plan on Gender Based Violence and Femicide: Human Dignity and Healing, Safety, Freedom and Equality in Our Lifetime." Youth and Persons with Disabilities (DWYPD) Department of Women. Pretoria, South Africa.

Dobash, R. Emerson, Russell P. Dobash, and Kate Cavanagh. 2009. "Out of the Blue" Men Who Murder an Intimate Partner." *Feminist Criminology* 4 (3):194–225. doi:10.1177/1557085109332668.

Fragoso, Julia Estela Monárrez. 2013. *Trama de una injusticia: feminicidio sexual sistémico en Ciudad Juárez*. Tijuana: El Colegio de la Frontera Norte.

García-Del Moral, Paulina. 2016. "Transforming Feminicidio: Framing, Institutionalization and Social Change." *Current Sociology* 64 (7):1017–1035. doi:10.1177/0011392115618731.

Gass, Jesse D., Dan J. Stein, David R. Williams, and Soraya Seedat. 2011. "Gender Differences in Risk for Intimate Partner Violence among South African Adults." *Journal of Interpersonal Violence* 26 (14):2764–2789. doi:10.1177/0886260510390960.

Gould, Chandre. 2015. "Beaten Bad-the Life Stories of Violent Offenders." *Institute for Security Studies Monographs* 2015 (192):1–144.

Government, South Africa. 1996. "The Constitution of the Republic of South Africa." Pretoria: South African Government.

Government of South Africa. 2020. "Emergency Response Action Plan to Address Gender Based Violence and Femicide." Government of South Africa, Pretoria.

Gupta, Neeru, and Mary Mahy. 2003. "Sexual Initiation among Adolescent Girls and Boys: Trends and Differentials in Sub-Saharan Africa." *Archives of Sexual Behavior* 32 (1):41–53. doi:10.1023/a:1021841312539.

Jewkes, Rachel, Yandisa Sikweyiya, Robert Morrell, and Kristin Dunkle. 2011. "The Relationship between Intimate Partner Violence, Rape and HIV Amongst South African Men: A Cross-Sectional Study." *PLoS ONE* 6 (9):e24256 doi:10.1371/journal.pone.0024256.

Long, J. W., K. Harper, D. Brennan, H. Harvey, R. Allen, K. Eliot, K. Ingala Smith, and C. O'Callaghan. 2020. "Femicide Census: UK Femicide 2009-2018." In *Femicide Census 10 Year Report*. London: Femicide Census.

Machisa, M., R. Jewkes, C. Lowe Morna, and K. Rama. 2011. "The WAR aT HOME: Gender Based Violence Indicators Project, Gauteng Research Report." Johannesburg, South Africa: Gender Links & South African Medical Research Council.

Mathews, Shanaaz, Rachel Jewkes, and Naeemah Abrahams. 2011. "I Had a Hard Life'Exploring Childhood Adversity in the Shaping of Masculinities among Men Who Killed an Intimate Partner in South Africa." *British Journal of Criminology* 51 (6): 960–977. doi:10.1093/bjc/azr051.

Mathews, Shanaaz, Rachel Jewkes, and Naeemah Abrahams. 2015. "So Now I'm the Man': Intimate Partner Femicide and Its Interconnections with Expressions of Masculinities in South Africa." *British Journal of Criminology* 55 (1):107–124. doi:10.1093/bjc/azu076.

McFarlane, Judith M., Jacquelyn C. Campbell, Susan Wilt, Carolyn J. Sachs, Yvonne Ulrich, and Xiao Xu. 1999. "Stalking and Intimate Partner Femicide." *Homicide Studies* 3 (4):300–316. doi:10.1177/1088767999003004003.

Monckton Smith, Jane. 2020. "Intimate Partner Femicide: Using Foucauldian Analysis to Track an Eight Stage Progression to Homicide." *Violence against Women* 26 (11): 1267–1285. doi:10.1177/1077801219863876.

National Department of Health (NDoH), Statistics South Africa (Stats SA), South African Medical Research Council (SAMRC), and ICF. 2019. "South Africa Demographic and Health Survey 2016." Pretoria South Africa: NDoH, Stats SA, SAMRC, and ICF.

Neumann, Pamela. 2022. "If It's Not Femicide, It's Still Murder": Contestations over Femicide in Nicaragua." *Feminist Criminology* 17 (1):139–159. doi:10.1177/15570851211037271.

Prinsloo, M., S. Mhlongo, B. Dekel, N. Gwebushe, L. Martin, G. Saayman, J. Vellema, et al. 2017. *The Injury Mortality Survey: A National Study of Injury Mortality Levels and Causes in South Africa in 2017*. Cape Town: South African Medical Research Council.

Richter, Linda, Musawenkosi Mabaso, Jordache Ramjith, and Shane A. Norris. 2015. "Early Sexual Debut: Voluntary or Coerced? Evidence from Longitudinal Data in South Africa–the Birth to Twenty plus Study." *South African Medical Journal* 105 (4):204–307. doi:10.7196/SAMJ.8925.

Russell, Diana E. H. 2012. "Defining Femicide." Discurso apresentado na abertura do Simpósio sobre Femicídio, das Nações Unidas em 26.

Sharps, Phyllis W., Jacquelyn Campbell, Doris Campbell, Fay Gary, and Daniel Webster. 2001. "The Role of Alcohol Use in Intimate Partner Femicide." *American Journal on Addictions* 10 (2):122–135.

Šimonović, D. 2020. "Intersection of Two Pandemics: COVID-19 and Violence against Women." UN Special Rapporteur on violence against women (A/75/144).

Šimonović, D. 2016. "Report of the Special Rapporteur on Violence against Women, Its Causes and Consequences." New York: UNGA, 71st Session.

Stöckl, Heidi, Ecaterina Balica, Consuelo Corradi, Anna Costanza Baldry, Monika Schröttle, Belén Sanz-Barbero, and Carmen Vives-Cases. 2020. "Issues in Measuring and Comparing the Incidence of Intimate Partner Homicide and Femicide-A Focus on Europe." *Rivista Sperimentale di Freniatria* (1):61–77. doi: 10.3280/RSF2020-001005.

Stöckl, Heidi, Karen Devries, Alexandra Rotstein, Naeemah Abrahams, Jacquelyn Campbell, Charlotte Watts, and Claudia Garcia Moreno. 2013. "The Global Prevalence of Intimate Partner Homicide: A Systematic Review." *The Lancet* 382 (9895):859–865. doi:10.1016/S0140-6736(13)61030-2.

United Nations Office on Drugs, and Crime. 2018. "Global Study on Homicide: Gender-Related Killing of Women and Girls." New York: UNODC, United Nations Office on Drugs and Crime.

Weil, Shalva. 2016. "Making Femicide Visible." *Current Sociology* 64 (7):1124–1137. doi:10.1177/0011392115623602.

Weil, Shalva, Consuelo Corradi, and Marceline Naudi. 2018. *Femicide across Europe: Theory, Research and Prevention*. Bristol: Policy Press.

Transitional Justice Interviews and Reflections: Perspectives of Women Survivors of the Rwandan Genocide against the Tutsi on Reparation and Repair

Noam Schimmel

THE RWANDAN GENOCIDE AGAINST THE TUTSI

The Rwandan genocide against the Tutsi began on April 7th of 1994 and ended on July 4rth that same year, one hundred days later. Over one million Tutsis were murdered in the genocide and tens of thousands of Hutus who rejected genocide and racism against Tutsis were massacred in the crime against humanity of extermination by the Hutu supremacist regime. The legacies of the genocide are still deeply felt in Rwanda today and in the Rwandan diaspora globally.

The voices of survivors of genocide and other mass atrocity have largely been elided in the extensive development of academic literature on transitional justice. With the aim of amplifying grassroots perspectives on transitional justice and, specifically, reparative justice, women survivors of the Rwandan genocide against the Tutsi were asked to share their reflections on this subject for this forthcoming special issue of Peace Review. Two contributors wish to remain anonymous and pseudonyms have been used for them to protect their privacy. The third, Jacqueline Murekatete, is the founder and director of the Brooklyn based Genocide Survivors Foundation, which works to secure the human rights and welfare of survivors of the genocide against the Tutsi, to educate about genocide, and to advocate for genocide prevention. She is married with two children, lives in New York City, and holds a BA in Politics from NYU and a JD from Benjamin Cardozo School of Law. The website of Genocide Survivors Foundation can be found at: https://genocidesurvivorsfoundation.org

All three survivors are active in human rights advocacy for Rwandan genocide survivors and expansion of opportunities to educate about the genocide, its historical antecedents in state-sanctioned anti-Tutsi discrimination and racism in Rwanda from 1959-1994, and in efforts to commemorate the victims of the genocide. Jacqueline Murekatete has lived in the United States since 1995. Her mother, father, six siblings, and most of her extended family were murdered in the genocide.

These are direct quotations of the commentaries they have provided. Interviewees were asked to address how they define reparative justice, what types of programs advance reparative justice, the rights and needs of women genocide survivors, the ways in which women experienced the genocide, and the consequences of the genocide and vulnerabilities and disadvantages that women genocide survivors face. Resilience, leadership, collective empowerment, healing, and rehabilitation are topics that survivors discussed in reflecting upon these topics and each of the interviewees themselves reflects an extraordinary capacity for resilience despite enormous adversity, loss, grief, and suffering. They demonstrate human rights leadership and advance empowerment of the survivor community, contributing to healing and rehabilitation both individually and collectively.

Femicide is frequently a feature of genocide, and this was particularly the case during the Rwandan genocide against the Tutsi in which Tutsi women were targeted for sexual violence on account of being both women and Tutsi. Rape and the deliberate infection of Tutsi women with HIV by Hutu genocidal militias was a central feature of the genocide, with the explicit aim of causing them a slow, wasting, tortuous death. The bodies of Tutsi women were mutilated during torture and after their deaths to magnify suffering for Tutsis individually and collectively, humiliate, degrade, devalue, and dehumanize them.

The genocide was characterized by sadistic brutality, and Tutsi men and women both experienced the most extreme forms of torture. Tutsi women were particularly targeted during the genocide because of hatred directed at them as Tutsi mothers who create, nurture, and protect Tutsi children and sustain the continuity of Tutsis as a community. They were also hated and attacked for their beauty, with many genocidal leaders hurling epithets about how their bodies would be disfigured and rendered ugly through rape and torture, to violate their dignity, stigmatize their Tutsiness, and mock them for their facial and other physical features. Many Tutsi women were considered to be particularly beautiful in Rwandan culture and this generated tremendous resentment amongst many Hutu men with Hutu supremacist beliefs, particularly those joining in the genocide. Many Tutsi women also chose to marry Tutsi men (although many married Hutus) and for marrying Tutsi men they were also hated. Precisely because femicide was such a central feature of the Rwandan genocide against the Tutsi, it is essential to listen to the voices of women survivors of the genocide to better understand femicide during genocide, its consequences, and how to better support and stand in solidarity with survivors of genocidal femicide and femicide in other contexts.

To better understand the role of femicide within the Rwandan genocide, I cite below three testimonies from women survivors of the genocide who reflected upon their experiences as women in a book compiled by the NGO SURF Survivor's Fund, "Survival Against the Odds: A Book of Testimonies from Survivors of the Rwandan Genocide." What emerges from each of these testimonies as they depict femicide during the genocide is a clear targeting of Tutsi women for being both women and Tutsi and a deliberate effort to harm, humiliate, degrade, torture, and dehumanize them for both being women and for being Tutsi and in ways that attack both their bodies and their spirits as women.

> They would pour beer for us to drink, mocking us that Tutsi women did not want them before, but now they were going to have us. Each took us in turns. My son tried to stop them, I suppose thinking he was going to die anyway. But they fought him off, hitting him with everything they had – masus, knives, sticks - until he died... Then they continued raping us. My daughters wanted to scream out in pain but were too scared to, so we remained quiet. My husband was forced to watch the whole ordeal. They didn't want to kill him quickly. They wanted him to watch, then die slowly. Helplessly, he watched them violating us. Then they hit him with a hammer on his head and back. He died the next day.

> The rape continued into the second day. I could not take it anymore. But when I tried to resist, they hit me on my arm and shoulder. Blood started flowing and the children began to scream. They attempted to run off but were stopped. They continued to rape my daughters too, saying they wanted to test Tutsi women. They then slashed me with a knife across my breast. Every so often they would take a break to drink whisky, which made them go even more crazy, as they took it in turns moved from one of us then to another... The housekeeper boasted about raping me – his employer – to the others. He knifed my privates after raping me.

> On the third day, they returned with a community officer. She said she was going to protect my girls. But when she left with the Interahamwe, I could hear them mocking me, saying they were taking them to be their wives. I was left alone. People would come

to the house, look at me and just leave. I had no-one to bring me water. I had no-one to help bury my husband and son. They told me they wanted to see how a Tutsi corpse decomposes. (Survival Against the Odds, SURF, 26 & 27).

Daphrosa

Thinking about the genocide, I sometimes think, at least my brother died immediately. My father had to watch us being raped and abused. My mother was raped, then my sister and then me. My father was forced to watch. He couldn't move, not even look away... While at home I was raped by four men. Here I was to be raped by another four men. I begged them to stop, but they refused. They said that we used to refuse Hutu men, and that now they have the right to do as they wished with us. They then took me to their command post, at a place they called Soferwa, where they did their killing. When we arrived they put me with street kids and delinquents, saying that they had brought them Tutsi women to test. They kept us there for one month, raping us and doing with us what they wanted. I was only 14 years old at the time. The Councillor's brother, Munana, was my old classmate. I begged him to keep me to himself, not allow me to be raped by everyone and anyone. But he didn't want anything more to do with me, so took me to find refuge at St. Famille Church. There were many refugees. Many Interahamwe made regular visits to this church. They came in large numbers, taking me and other women out of the church to rape us. I lost count how many times this happened. I can't even begin to explain. This went on for two months. The Interahamwe would bring soldiers who were manning the roadblock, to show them stubborn Tutsi women who refused to have a Hutu man. They gave me to seven soldiers, who all raped me until they had enough of me. (Survival Against the Odds, SURF, 30 & 31).

Aline

Before they killed my wife, they raped her. I saw it all. They gang-raped her. I managed to see five men, after which I could not see. My senses failed me. I fell unconscious. My youngest child, whom she was breastfeeding, was torn from her and smashed against a wall and died straight away. My other child rubbed his fingers begging for mercy and pardon, as if he had done something wrong. A group of Interahamwe hacked him to pieces with machetes. He too died. After they had raped my wife, they began debating who should take her home for a wife. They decided that all should have a piece of her. One man cut her arm off, and one the other. They tore her to shreds so that no-one could have her. Every day, many women and girls were raped. Some were spared as future wives, but many were killed after the sexual ordeal. No-one would say anything. It was time to die. Families could only watch helplessly as their loved ones cried out for mercy or help. (Survival Against the Odds, SURF, 36).

- Feridina

INTERVIEW QUESTIONS

Interviewees were given the following list of questions and had the option of answering some or all of them, as well as adding their own reflections and comments.

1. What are the necessary components of restorative/reparative justice for women survivors?
2. How can development NGOs working in Rwanda address the needs and human rights of women genocide survivors more effectively?
3. How were the experiences of women genocide survivors during the genocide different from those of men? What are their particular needs as a result, particularly regarding health and trauma reduction support services?
4. What are concerns that you have that you wish to share about the challenges that you face as a woman genocide survivor?
5. How have women survivors worked together to advance their rights and welfare both within Rwanda and in the Rwandan diaspora?
6. How should women's rights and welfare organizations working in Rwanda, such as UN Women, the Global Fund for Women, and Women for Women International support women genocide survivors?
7. Did the FARG (former Rwandan government agency charged with providing genocide survivors with a very limited amount of support for some of their needs) help women genocide survivors sufficiently? If not, how and why not? How can this be rectified by the Rwandan government and humanitarian aid and development agencies working in Rwanda?
8. How can men show solidarity with and support for women survivors of the genocide?

9. Please share any additional thoughts, concerns, and reflections that you have as a woman survivor of the genocide against the Tutsi.

JEANETTE

Trauma counseling is very important. If you are not stable mentally it's so hard to survive and be strong and move forward. There was no such thing as reparation in my country. People need to be empowered financially. People need to be seen and heard. There is so much silencing. People have no voice. You lost your family, your home, every person you love in the entire world and then you are there and nobody wants to listen to you and you are just a complainer and nobody wants to listen to you. It is terrible and sad what is happening in the survivor's lives.

When you see the homes where survivors of genocide live now and their homes were destroyed during the genocide even if they live in those little homes that they were given, some of them are homeless, they are hungry. I am pretty sure there is a way they could receive a home and help.

The UN needs to do something. Those countries who played a role during the genocide should do something for survivors of genocide, especially France. France was hand in hand with Habyarimana's government in preparation for genocide and during the genocide as well. It won't bring back what survivors have lost, but at least to do something, that would be helpful in one way or another.

Education is very important. When you say now education is free education was never free in our country and probably will never be free. Survivors of genocide should at least receive free education so that they can be free financially.

I think development NGOs need to be listening and doing some research. If they don't know the stories of survivors and don't know how they are struggling and what are their basic needs and what they need most and the due diligence of how their money will be used then there's no need to say they are helping survivors when really they are not. They have not researched who needs the money most. They need to speak to survivors of genocide to figure out if the money they are giving to Rwanda and to survivors of the genocide is doing what it's supposed to be doing. People are struggling, still hungry, and have no food and no homes.

It was unspeakable what happened to ladies during the genocide. Rape which sometimes we don't talk about in our culture. We still have people who were raped in the genocide who don't talk about it because of the shame that it brings them. When it comes to pain everyone's experience was terrible. I don't know how to compare pain. Those external and internal wounds they still see and feel, especially when you see those with HIV today. I have a friend who is a survivor of genocide who was raped who says that every time she takes that pill (antiretroviral) it takes her back to what she went through during the genocide. We have so many ladies who live through those moments because of those internal and external wounds that they still see with their eyes.

When you destroy women you destroy the family. And that is the case in our country where survivors of genocide, women, a lot of them were destroyed. The percentage of people who say they were raped is not an accurate percentage for sure... (Not all women share that they were raped.)

'Therapy is needed in our country. Those rape survivors are wounded. And it will be a circle of psychological problems because the pain they carry will be transmitted and passed on to their kids and it will effect the generation to come if not treated. When I look around, it is not being treated enough. There is a lot to be done. People say it has been 27 years... When it comes to trauma and pain there is no timeframe for getting better. Everyone is different.

CHRISTINE

Prosecution of the killers of their families is part of reparative justice. Serious measures need to be taken to prevent those who still want to kill or harass the survivors from being able to achieve their desires. The lives &families and pets as well as belongings of genocide survivors all have to be respected.

Development NGOs should take time to sit with survivors and identify their needs as there are many different people amongst the survivors with different lifestyles, different issues depending on what they endured - especially getting to talk directly to them helps with getting accurate information on what their needs really are.

Genocide survivors were dehumanized: abused sometimes in front of their kids' eyes; they were tortured beyond understanding like mutilation, ... They need counseling, sustainable daily basic needs (food, housing, transportation and financial support) to put food on the table for their families and themselves, they need empathy through talking it out and care, medical attention, accommodation and help from doctors to encourage healthy eating to fight diseases triggered by serious sickness they got from the abuse they experienced during the genocide.

Genocide survivors have been a voice to the voiceless, organizing fundraisers toward the education of the survivors, education and medical expenses! Many are trying to lend a hearing ear to the oppressed. They also wrote books to raise awareness of the Genocide against Tutsis, attended important conferences, spreading the word as much as possible. They also engage in storytelling to heal themselves.

Aid agencies need to show them that they are not alone, they need visits, people to check on their kids and assist them while they are living with serious illnesses. They need help with seeking medical attention with funding the projects that can lead to financial self-sufficiency (this would bring hope and less worries that can bring setbacks and flashbacks of the worst past.)

FARG (former Rwandan agency providing assistance to genocide survivors) did not help enough because genocide survivors are still dealing with the aftermath of the genocide. For example, the houses built for them some are in bad quality, they are still struggling with basic needs. The Rwandan government needs to approach genocide survivors and spot their concerns to get more accurate information and know more of where the help is needed.

The stories of all the victims and what they were put through cannot be forgotten like frying kids on the pans ... Survivors would be considered as fragile humans who experienced much, those who kill their pets or try to go back to kill the survivors should be punished seriously as an example to others.

JACQUELINE MUREKATETE

I think the first thing development NGOs working in Rwanda need to take into account is that genocide survivors have unique needs as a result of their genocide experience that cannot/should never be put in the same basket as the needs of Rwandans generally. The most common mistake NGOs make is to view/treat genocide survivors' needs under the larger umbrella of development, poverty reduction, and the like and as a result these NGOs too often fail to allocate specific funding that is specifically tailored to survivors unique needs.

In failing to acknowledge that survivors' needs are not general but unique and intricately tied to the pain, suffering and loss caused by the Genocide, survivors' unique needs are often overlooked or only addressed at the surface level, leaving survivors with a lack of acknowledgement, loneliness and a sense of abandonment once again.

Women genocide survivors as a sub-group of genocide survivors also have specific needs that are unique to them as a result of their gender. Development NGO's must always remember that women and girls were not only targets for murder during the genocide, but they were also more often than men made to be the victims of rape, sexual slavery and other gender-based violence. As such, women survivors today not only have to cope with the loss of their loved ones and the overall pain and trauma caused by the genocide that male survivors have to deal with, but many of the women survivors also live with the physical and emotional wounds caused by the gender based violence experienced during the genocide. Development NGOs in Rwanda must therefore take all this in consideration and allocate specific and tailored funding to address the gender specific harms suffered by women genocide survivors.

Finally, funding or any other support to address the unique needs of genocide survivors generally or women genocide survivors specifically should be channeled through local survivors organizations/associations and should always be in partnership with them as these organizations/associations are best situated to understand and meet the needs of fellow survivors.

Tutsi women and girls during the genocide were not only targeted for systematic murder, as their male counterparts were, but they were also too often victims of multiple rapes and other forms of gender-based violence. As a result many of them now live with the physical consequences of that gender based violence including HIV/AIDS, paralysis, inability to bear children and other profound physical disabilities. Women genocide survivors also live with emotional and psychological wounds caused by the gender- based violence they suffered which is further compounded by the stigmatization and social isolation that many of them often experience. Thus, women genocide survivors need comprehensive services including economic support, educational support, healthcare services to address the physical wounds and illnesses they face today as a result of the gender-based violence they suffered as well as psychological/mental health support services to help them cope with the profound trauma that they live with.

In addition to the general challenges and daily struggles that I face by the nature of being a genocide survivor, there are also specific challenges that I and other women genocide survivors face at different stages of our lives by the nature of us being women genocide survivors. One challenge/painful reality that has become even more profound for me lately for example, is the absence of my mother to provide the support and guidance that I need as a young mother today. For those of us who were young girls during the genocide, we were not only deprived of our mothers by the genocide, but we were also robbed of a mother's wisdom and guidance which every young girl needs as she progress from girlhood to womanhood to motherhood.

In a world where it is more than true that it takes a village to raise a child, many young mothers like myself today are often forced to deal with the painful fact that the people who constituted our village-our mothers, aunts and other women relatives etc ... were brutally taken away from us by genocide and we must navigate the journey of motherhood today with a lot of joy yes but always with a certain level of loneliness, pain and a profound sense of loss.

I think some of the ways that men can show solidarity with and support for women survivors is to lend them a listening ear, to refrain from stigmatizing and isolating the women and girls who were victims of rape and other gender-based violence during the genocide and to be their allies/support system in their daily struggles including in their fight/search for justice for the gender specific harms suffered during the genocide.

REFLECTIONS ON THE INTERVIEWS

A primary concern of all three survivors interviewed is the lack of support for the respect and fulfillment of the human rights of genocide survivors and a lack of inclusion of genocide survivors in benefitting from development and humanitarian aid in Rwanda. Although there is a large presence of development and humanitarian aid NGOs in Rwanda including many that focus on women's rights and that incorporate concern for the respect, protection, and fulfillment of women's rights in their programming – they do not significantly address women genocide survivors. Despite advocacy on the part of women genocide survivors urging these NGOs to center women survivors of the genocide in their programming, NGOs have overwhelmingly marginalized women survivors for reasons of political expedience and because of a general unwillingness to acknowledge the unique and severe forms of vulnerability and disadvantage that women genocide survivors in Rwanda face. We see the concern the survivors interviewed here have with this systemic institutionalized injustice, with Jacqueline Murekatete addressing it in particular depth and detail. As a founder of the Genocide Survivors Foundation in her advocacy work she has seen over and over again the extent to which genocide survivors – and especially women genocide survivors – are marginalized and excluded in the context of development and humanitarian aid in Rwanda and in the values and practices of international NGOs and national aid agencies and UN agencies working in Rwanda.

Key concerns that the interviewees highlight that need to be taken into account and responded to by human rights, development, and humanitarian aid NGOs in Rwanda and by binational and international aid agencies such as USAID and United Nations agencies such as UNDP, UNICEF, and UN Women include:

- Psychological and trauma support services including comprehensive counseling, social worker, and therapeutic interventions to address anxiety, hopelessness, isolation, depression, and trauma
- Recognition of the profound and complex ways in which women survivors of genocide experience deprivation as a result of the genocide and its legacy
- Recognition of and responsiveness to the unique needs and vulnerabilities of genocide survivors – specifically women survivors – and substantive and sustained efforts to work closely with genocide survivor organizations as full partners in development and humanitarian aid that is inclusive of genocide survivors and that values and affirms their right to consultation, participation, and partnership
- Medical care, especially medical care that is gender sensitive and responsive
- Financial support including job training and training and support for income-generating activities
- Addressing food insecurity with reliable, sufficient, and nutritious food provision
- Adequate provision of safe shelter
- Support for the education of genocide survivors, both formal school and technical-vocational training and other forms of education that advance self-empowerment, self-reliance, and full social and economic integration
- Accountability for and reparative justice from governments such as the French government that were complicit in the genocide and for organizations who were complicit as well, such as the United Nations
- Retributive justice for those individuals who participated in the genocide, whatever their background and nationality
- Public education and commemoration of the genocide

Unfortunately, it is rare that one finds the voices of women genocide survivors and genocide survivors in Rwanda more broadly in the development, humanitarian aid, and human rights literature on Rwanda. This article aims to plant a seed in the hope of stimulating greater attention to the human rights, needs, realities, perspectives, and hopes of Rwanda's genocide survivors and in particular of women survivors.

Although there is a fairly small literature on women's experiences of femicide during the genocide, it is growing. 28 years after the genocide more women survivors are publishing memoirs, testimonies, and providing interviews in which they share and reflect upon their experiences being targeted as Tutsi women during the genocide. This is an encouraging development, and one which allows for greater insight and understanding of women's experiences of the genocide and of the ways in which femicide was a specific feature of the Rwandan genocide against the Tutsi, an emphasis of the genocide's organizers and implementers, and which has had severe and challenging consequences for women survivors of the genocide, as the interviewees discuss.

Reclaiming the dignity of their being women, their bodily and psychological and physical integrity and security of person and of spirit, and restoring the place of Tutsi women within Rwandan society as being rights-bearing and worthy of respect are of urgent importance. So too is improving their place in Rwandan society in a more emancipatory direction that demands greater equality and justice for them and for all Rwandan women.

Rehabilitation, reparation, and collective empowerment of women survivors requires a fundamental paradigm shift in the values, policies, and practices of humanitarian and development NGOs in Rwanda, bilateral and multilateral aid agencies, and agencies of the United Nations. That 28 years after the genocide Rwanda's women survivors remain marginalized illustrates the way in which women survivors of femicide during the genocide are disadvantaged because of systemic failures to respect and fulfill their human rights, with the resulting injustices and inequalities these interviews reveal and which these survivors explain need to be urgently addressed and rectified. I am deeply grateful for the trust placed in me in sharing their testimonies. It is with great respect and profound admiration for their commitment to justice and collective empowerment for Rwanda's genocide survivors and for women survivors in particular that I share their concerns and commentaries. Murakoze cyane. (Thank you in Kinyarwanda.)

Femicide has devastating consequences. But Rwanda's women genocide survivors are immensely powerful. Their testimonies illustrate their fortitude and capacity for renewal, individual and collective resilience, and an undeterred spirit that humbles, inspires, and creates hope and light. With defiance, dignity, and deep affirmation of their value, wisdom, and promise Rwanda's women genocide survivors are healing, rebuilding, and sharing their stories of survival, strength, and the solace they find in one another and in mutual and collective empowerment.

FOR MORE ON THE EXPERIENCES OF WOMEN SURVIVORS OF THE RWANDAN GENOCIDE AGAINST THE TUTSI SEE

de Brouwer, Anne-Marie, Sandra Ka Hon Chu, Eef je de Volder, and Samer Muscati. 2019. *And I Live On: The Resilience of Rwandan Survivors of Sexual Violence*. Nijmegen: Wolf Press.

Jean, Hatzfeld. 2007. *Life Laid Bare: The Survivors in Rwanda Speak*. New York City: The Other Press.

Kagoyire, M., and A. Richters. 2018. ""We Are the Memory Representation of Our Parents": Intergenerational Legacies of Genocide among Descendants of Rape Survivors in Rwanda." *Torture: Quarterly Journal on Rehabilitation of Torture Victims and Prevention of Torture* 28 (3) :30–45. doi: 10.7146/torture.v28i3.111183.

Magill, Christine, and Ferguson Will. 2019. *The Hope That Remains: Canadian Survivors of the Rwandan Genocide*. Montreal: Vehicule Press.

Mukamana, D., and P. Brysiewicz. 2008. "The Lived Experience of Genocide Rape Survivors in Rwanda." *Journal of Nursing Scholarship : An Official Publication of Sigma Theta Tau International Honor Society of Nursing* 40 (4) :379–384. doi: 10.1111/j.1547-5069.2008.00253.x.

Sinalo, Caroline. 2019. *Rwanda after Genocide: Gender, Identity, and Post-Traumatic Growth*. Cambridge: Cambridge University Press.

Survival Against the Odds. *A Book of Testimonies from Survivors of the Rwandan Genocide*. SURF, Survivor's Fund.

The testimonies and reports of SURF Survivor's Fund. Available at: https://survivors-fund.org.uk/learn/testimonies/; https://survivors-fund.org.uk/learn/survival-against-the-odds/; https://survivors-fund.org.uk/about/our-reports/annual-reports/

Zraly, M., and L. Nyirazinyoye. 2010. "Don't Let the Suffering Make You Fade Away: An Ethnographic Study of Resilience among Survivors of Genocide-Rape in Southern Rwanda." *Social Science & Medicine* 70 (10):1656–1664. doi: 10.1016/j.socscimed.2010.01.017.

Zraly, Maggie, Julia Rubin-Smith, and Theresa Betancourt. 2011. "Primary Mental Health Care for Survivors of Collective Sexual Violence in Rwanda." *Global Public Health* 6 (3):257–270. doi: 10.1080/17441692.2010.493165.

Suicide, Femicide, and COVID-19

KATERINA STANDISH

Suicide is a deliberate act of violence that can be considered the ultimate form of self-destruction. To take one's own life, is an eradication of potential, the obliteration of existence, and the number one form of violent death worldwide. Far surpassing the number of victims who die from conflict, civil war, or terrorism, suicide, whether medical or instrumental, is the most prevalent incarnation of violent death in most nations and claims upwards of a million people a year. Femicide, the deliberate killing of a person because they are female is a form of homicide that frequently happens in the home, by a current or past intimate partner and, like suicide, is also a pandemic—causing (pre-COVID-19) over 90,000 victims a year.

A social fact is a result of some form of human interaction, activity or deed—not a conscious intention so much as an effect or outcome of human activity. Social facts are therefore unintended circumstances that come to exert power over individuals and constrain them. The social facts of suicide and femicide will both be deeply impacted by the novel coronavirus. As social circumstances change as a consequence of the global COVID-19 illness the worldwide actions of addressing the disease will lead to unanticipated suicidal and femicidal consequences; and furthermore, domestic responses to COVID-19 will both constrain and compel these forms of preventable violence for the near future. This essay seeks to elevate our perception of the conflict of the COVID-19 crisis in relation to two often invisible forms of violence exacerbated by the global response to the pandemic: suicide and femicide.

The novel coronavirus that causes the COVID-19 infection first surfaced in China in December of 2019. Since then the global spread of the illness has caused widespread disruption in human living systems including employment, subsistence and public health. As Anand Lingeswaran and Mark Reger et al., point out, globally, threats to individual mental health have spiked since February of 2020 resulting in elevated distress levels contributing to anxiety, depression, insecurity and social isolation. The circumstances of lock-down, quarantine, social distancing and pervasive economic and social disorder create a perfect-storm of stress, substance abuse, loneliness, sleeplessness, grief, anger, hopelessness, and trauma.

As resources get channeled toward the virus, the risks of deliberate self-killing (suicide) as a result of unprecedented levels of stress, diminished social support, and lethal gender-based violence (GBV) against women in isolation (femicide), means the world appears to be addressing one threat while increasing the risks of two others. The pandemic will increase violence against women (VAW) and lead to a wave of suicide. Suicide is normally expected to follow the illness, similar to pandemics of the past such as SARS, HINI, and the Spanish Flu epidemic of 1918. Accounts of suicide spikes "during" the pandemic, however, have now been reported in the UK, Europe, Asia, and the U.S. with some increases up 70% from last year. At the time of writing, lockdown related femicide, predictable yet invisible, is cohabiting many spaces designed to remedy the pandemic.

In Spain, there were 18 femicide fatalities from the beginning of 2020 until mid-March, several of them having occurred during the Coronavirus outbreak. In Argentina, where the rate of femicide is extraordinarily high during regular times, 86 femicides have already been perpetrated since the beginning of 2020, of which 24 occurred during the Covid-19 plague. The Argentinian Femicide Observatory ("Now that they See Us") reported that one woman was killed every 29 hours during March 2020. In Turkey, 18 women have been killed since the lockdown has been instituted, the majority in their homes. In Israel, there have been six cases of femicide since January 2020, three of them during the Coronavirus outbreak. In the urge to stay alive, people will face unparalleled risk and many will die, not from the novel coronavirus, but from public health initiatives intended to tackle it.

Suicide can be separated into two categories: medical and instrumental. Medical suicide involves individuals and contains the most prevalent form of suicide—suicide related to mental illness—as well as assisted suicide and euthanasia. Instrumental suicide involves other people and includes suicide attacks, homicide-suicides (including femicide), daredevil suicides, and protest suicides. Suicides are deeply gendered forms of violence and include males and females in diverse and divergent patterns. Roughly 75% of suicidal violence is completed by men and boys whereas suicide attempts are conducted most frequently by women and girls. Suicidal ideation, imagining a deliberate life-ending act is a key facet of suicidality—a propensity toward suicidal violence—and relates to age, gender, and access to support services. As females are more prone to suicidal ideation their utilization of support services is directly associated with both the creation of suicide plans and suicide attempts. As more men and boys die by suicidal violence, and circumstances that lead to increased suicidality will intensify during the lockdown, we can expect to see increasing levels of both attempted suicide and completed suicide related to the pandemic.

Although there are at minimum seven different categories of suicide identified in recent scholarship, the form of suicide most prevalent and most impacted by the circumstances of the pandemic (and the global response) is medical suicide related to mental illness. Mental illness relates to recognizable mood disorders including depression, anxiety, bipolar disease, and schizophrenia but also substance abuse problems from intoxicants such as drugs and alcohol. Considering that 90% of completed suicides were suffering from a mental disorder when they died, the impact of mental wellness on deliberate self-killing is unquestionable.

During normal (non-pandemic) times, the number of people suffering from mood disorders is considerable and many do not have access to quality and consistent care. During COVID-19 the number of people suffering from social, psychological, and biological stress is skyrocketing, many will be unable to function and will experience incapacity from low moods that reduce life enjoyment, future (hopeful) mindedness, and emotional resilience. The physiological symptoms of fatigue, sleeplessness, lack of focus, and feelings of despair, grief, loneliness and worthlessness will increase and lead to physical symptoms of unwellness exacerbated by limited and triaged healthcare.

Many physicians and nurses are already at their edge of being able to function on the front line due to the workload and misery of caring for patients suffering in isolation and great pain. More and more people delay or are unable to receive medical attention for non-COVID-19 related concerns as fear of health-care facilities, including hospitals and clinics, but also, fear of leaving home bubbles, makes taking care of existing and escalating health matters an obstacle that can have lethal outcomes. For differently abled and chronically ill people the barrier to sustainable and available health care may be unmanageable to ascend. The response to COVID-19 means that most other health concerns (whether physical or mental) are being triaged and this lacuna of care is expected to last for the duration of this pandemic, a timeline that could possibly be years.

There are two contemporary responses to suicidal violence that can be identified in the literature: the medical model and the social model. Due to the 19th and 20th Century medicalization of suicide, the predominant belief that it is a psychological (mental) or biomedical (genetic) malady and the perception that suicidal behavior is pathologically related to mental unwellness, the medical model addresses suicidality with medication and therapy. This approach is focused on individuals and typically includes methods that identify the need for increases in service delivery of mental health. The medical approach has been criticized by suicidologists who highlight that the pathologization of suicide means that increased psychotherapeutic and medical tactics limit alternative prevention approaches and necessitate so-called scientific models of ameliorative address.

In contrast, the social model identifies suicidal violence within a web of social determinants like unemployment, experiences of trauma and abuse (especially in childhood), history of social or geographic isolation (including the breakdown of social networks), chronic illness, and social (relational) insecurity. The social model identifies stressors related to financial stress, unemployment or underemployment, relationship breakdown, and potential legal challenges. As the social model sees the causes of depression as social it therefore considers the social self in addressing potential suicidal violence. The social model incorporates the social or environmental aspects that surround an individual and support mechanisms such as employment, sense of belonging and care are examined and deployed.

The reality of COVID-19 means that both the baseline of mental illness (levels of depression, anxiety, bipolar disorder, schizophrenia, and substance abuse problems) and the surrounding circumstantial threats of financial stress, unemployment, relationship breakdowns, and domestic stress including insecurity, precarity, and isolation will escalate. The conditions that result from a public response to the novel coronavirus mean that the threat of suicide will only grow during lockdowns and as previous pandemics have shown, likely lead to a surge of post-pandemic suicides the world over. The pandemic will initially suppress suicides but afterward, suicidal violence will form a demographic wave seen worldwide. In pandemic times both the medical model and social model of addressing, suppressing and preventing suicidal violence, for different reasons, become untenable.

The pandemic is gendered. While many men will experience the illness and the economic and social ramifications, post-pandemic realities will see men return to pre-pandemic life. Women however, are overwhelmed with domestic burdens, front-line and essential service work and experience abuse and levels of stress unremittingly since the start of the virus. Shelter-in-place, seclusion, lockdown, or bubble orders that require people to remain sequestered where they live are societal responses to the epidemiological threat of the novel coronavirus, but in these so-called safe spaces, another threat is amplified, one of violence against women, and one that predictably results in the deliberate killing of women by men.

Femicide is a form of violence against women and can be defined as killing of a woman or girl because of their gender. Femicide was defined at the United Nations Commission on Crime Prevention and Criminal Justice as: first, the murder of women as a result of domestic violence/intimate partner violence; second, the torture and misogynist slaying of women; third, killing of women and girls in the name of "honour"; fourth, targeted killing of women and girls in the context of armed conflict; fifth, dowry-related killings of women and girls; sixth, killing of women and girls because of their sexual orientation and gender identity; seventh, the killing of aboriginal and indigenous women and girls because of their gender; eighth, female infanticide and gender-based sex selection feticide; ninth, genital mutilation related femicide; tenth, accusations of witchcraft; and eleventh, other femicides connected with gangs, organized crime, drug dealers, human trafficking, and the proliferation of small arms.

While male homicides occur in public, female homicide (femicide) occurs in the domestic sphere, is largely perpetrated by men (past or present partners), and is the culmination of ongoing abuse, threats, intimidation, and sexual violence. Femicide, because it occurs largely in the private sphere, is both less visible and more difficult to address under cultural, legal, social and situational parameters. Because violence against women is condoned, excused and legitimate in many social spaces, femicide, as the culmination of forced proximity due to lockdown is woefully predictable. As women remain confined to home spaces with abusive partners because of the pandemic response, it comes as no surprise that globally there has been a steep rise in reporting of domestic violence. A recent UNWOMEN focus piece entitled *The Shadow Pandemic: Violence Against Women During COVID-19* avers that, "[s]ince the outbreak of COVID-19, emerging data and reports from those on the front lines, have shown that all types of violence against women and girls, particularly domestic violence, has intensified." Furthermore, the inability for women to access shelter and support mean that many women live in a world of constant fear where the response to COVID-19 forces them to remain in spaces of constant and compounding violence.

Responses to femicide are fragmented and ineffectual. The phenomenon of femicide (only formally recognized in the 1990s as a distinct form of violence based on the identity of the victim as opposed to the "action" or crime committed) is approached from a criminological standpoint after violence has occurred, from an anthropological standpoint as a form of social dominance, and from a sociological standpoint as the result of social circumstances that permit the killing of women. Support and rescue for those at risk of femicide is victim sourced, trivialized, stigmatized, and inefficient. The cultural and social support of femicide as a result of male supremacy relegates the experience of this worldwide form of violence invisible or legitimate which, similar to other group targeted forms of violence, such as genocide, mires the eradication of femicide in policy and intention rather than consideration and attention.

The threatening and horrific experiences of women, women now forced to remain in violent living spaces with dangerous men, is not only an unconsidered aspect of the pandemic response but a marker of the ongoing inability for nations to prioritize the safety of women in policy. Violence against women, which culminates in their death at the hands of men, is largely unexamined in existing social orders that speak of gender equality while continuing to uphold patriarchal privileges.

Violence is the primary marker of the discipline of Peace and Conflict Studies; the absence, presence, and substance of violence defines the field and its descriptive and prescriptive avenues of appreciation. While Johan Galtung provided a framework of violence to include cultural, structural (indirect), and direct forms, he curiously neglected to include violence against women within his violence strata. Galtung manages to erase gender in his categories of structural and direct violence (aggressions against survival, well-being, identity, and freedom needs) but when he examines the ideological facets chosen and un-chosen-ness, he identifies male supremacy (being chosen by an Abrahamic deity) as resulting in (only) two outcomes: sexism, Witch-burning.

As the United Nations Commission on Crime Prevention and Criminal Justice assert, there are forms of violence perpetrated against women that men do not experience. Femicide is violence against women—because they are women. Neglecting violence against women in Galtung's theory does more than collapse the experience of violence, it erases it. And considering that his theory formally presents a temporal consideration of violence—that cultural violence (worldviews) leads to structural (systemic) and direct (incidental) forms—the invisibility of violence against women, because they are women, perpetuates male power over women. Sexism, as a system of male supremacy is never tied to the tangible experience of how women experience such violence (sexism is not a form of violence—it is violence) as oppressive, repressive, exploitative, diminishing, maiming, subordinating, lethal as it is used as a tool by men to keep women afraid, dependent, subservient, and ultimately, under male control. And while individual acts of violence by males against women are forms of direct violence, the situation of male supremacy worldwide, is cultural and both legitimizes and perpetuates femicide.

When Galtung considered cultural violence, he declared that one method of enabling it was to make the reality of violence opaque, so we either don't see or don't think what we see is violence. In the case of COVID-19, what we see is the human instrument as a vector of a potentially deadly pathogen who must be contained, controlled, and isolated to kill the disease (a virus needs a host or it does not reproduce). What we don't see, is the forthcoming wave of suicide just around the corner that will directly result from both the stress and grief of experiencing the pandemic (both the illness and the public response to it) and the social devastation of forced isolation, unemployment, inability to move in human spaces with physical connection, and the new-normal of somatic distancing. What we don't see as violence is the existing and exacerbating occurrence of femicide that will not only continue during the pandemic but will inevitably, predictably and sorrowfully increase.

In this essay I have humbly sought to speak for the dead—the dying, those who want to die, and those who will be killed because they are not men. The reality of the COVID-19 pandemic can be medically surveyed and epidemiologically considered but the human reaction to the disease will not only result in pandemic response protocols and hopefully decreasing numbers of infected and affected it will result in worldwide violence.

While many nations have yet to respond to the adjacent pandemics of suicide and femicide, some countries are striving to. For example, Norway immediately instituted measures of psycho-social support in their pandemic response that included financial support, crisis lines, and online service and treatment. In New Zealand, front line and health professionals are afforded counseling at no cost during COVID-19, and the "Getting Through Together" campaign is delivered to support the mental health of all New Zealanders. In Japan, recognition of domestic violence (DV) led to the creation of the *All Japan Women's Shelter Network* to provide counseling, protection, support, shelter, and financial payments to victims of DV, and the United Nations Democracy Fund (UNDEP) call for action against domestic violence during COVID-19 has resulted in media campaigns, help-lines, education, and advocacy in 15 nations.

Facing the threat of suicidal and femicidal violence means combining the medical and social models: tackling psychological health, and economic security in line with physical health. It also means making violence against women visible and creating public health responses that incorporate domestic violence into pandemic responses. COVID-19 is a social fact, the result of human activity that restrains and constrains individuals.

Suicide and femicide are social facts whose incidences are impacted by cultural, social, economic, political, and global circumstances. Prioritizing the pandemic over other social facts means prioritizing an economic and social system of wellness over the health and safety of women and girls, and those at current and future risk of suicidal violence. Femicide and suicide may be unintended outcomes of the COVID-19 pandemic but unless we prioritize a global response to these insidious and invisible forms of violence too, we may save the body but kill the person.

RECOMMENDED READINGS

Chan, Sau, M., S. Fung, K. H. Chiu, Chiu, W. L. Lam, P. Y. V. Leung, and Yeates Conwell. 2006. "Elderly Suicide and the 2003 SARS Epidemic in Hong Kong." *International Journal of Geriatric Psychiatry* 21 (2):113–118. doi: 10.1002/gps.1432.

Guntuku, Shravankumar. 2020. "The Need for Shift in Approach to Suicide Prevention in Australia." *Open Journal of Social Sciences* 8 (8):150–157. doi: 10.4236/jss.2020.88013.

Laurent, Claire, Michael Platzer, and Maria Idomir. 2013. *Femicide: A Global Issue That Demands Action.* Vienna: Academic Council on the United Nations System (ACUNS).

Lingeswaran, Anand. 2020. "Suicide Related Risk Factors during the COVID-19 Pandemic." *Paripex-Indian Journal of Research* 9 (8).

Liu, Xinhua, Meghana Kakade, Cordelia Fuller, Bin J. Fan, Yunyun Fang, Junhui Kong, Zhiquiang Guan, and Ping Wu. 2012. "Depression after Exposure to Stressful Events: Lessons Learned from the Severe Acute Respiratory Syndrome Epidemic." *Comprehensive Psychiatry* 53 (1):15–23. doi: 10.1016/j.comppsych.2011.02.003.

Lingeswaran, Anand. 2020. "Suicide Related Risk Factors during the COVID-19 Pandemic." *Paripex-Indian Journal of Research* 9 (8).

March, Ian. 2016. "Critiquing Contemporary Suicidology," in Jennifer White, Ian Marsh, Michael J. Kral, and Jonathan Morris (eds.), *Critical Suicidology: Transforming Suicide Research and Prevention for the 21st Century*, 15–30. Vancouver: UBC Press.

Miller, Eric D. 2020. "The COVID-19 Pandemic Crisis: The Loss and Trauma Event of Our Time." *Journal of Loss and Trauma* 25 (6-7):560–572. doi: 10.1080/15325024.2020.1759217.

Phillips, Michael. 2010. "Rethinking the Role of Mental Illness in Suicide." *American Journal of Psychiatry* 167 (7):731–733. doi: 10.1176/appi.ajp.2010.10040589.

Polischuk, Luciana, and Daniel L. Fay. 2020. "Administrative Response to Consequences of COVID-19 Emergency Responses: Observations and Implications from Gender-Based Violence in Argentina." *The American Review of Public Administration* 50 (6-7): 675–684. doi: 10.1177/0275074020942081.

Pridmore, William, and Pridmore Saxby. 2016. "Suicide is Not the Exclusive Domain of Medicine." *American Journal of Medical Research* 3 (1):174–187.

Raman, Sandhya. 2020. "Pandemic's effect on already rising suicide rates heightens worry." Available at: <https://medicalxpress.com/news/2020-08-pandemic-effect-suicide-heightens.html>.

Reger, Mark A., Ian H. Stanley, and Thomas E. Joiner. 2020. "Suicide Mortality and Coronavirus Disease 2019—a Perfect Storm?" *JAMA Psychiatry April Psychiatry* 77 (11):1093. doi: 10.1001/jamapsychiatry.2020.1060.

Sher, L. 2020. "The Impact of the COVID-19 Pandemic on Suicide Rates." *QJM (October 1)* 113 (10):707–712. doi: 10.1093/qjmed/hcaa202.

Standish, Katerina. 2020. *Suicide through a Peacebuilding Lens*. Singapore: Palgrave MacMillan.

Wasserman Ian, M. 1992. "The Impact of Epidemic, War, Prohibition and Media on Suicide: United States, 1910-1920." *Suicide & Life-Threatening Behavior* 22 (2): 240–254.

Weil, Shalva. 2020. "Gendering-Coronavirus (Covid-19) and Femicide." *European Sociologist* 45 (1):1–4.

Index

Note: **Bold** page numbers refer to tables and page numbers followed by "n" denote endnotes.

Abrahams, N. 84
Africa 4, 5, 81–91
agents 8, 12, 14, 15, 61
Alkire, Sabina 20
armed conflict 3, 4, 19, 20, 22, 24, 26, 32, 35, 39, 67

Badian, S. 89
Ball, Patrick 33n8, 36, 39n14
Barraza, Rodríguez 66
Bird, Sheila M. 39n14
birth-machines 10
Black Lives Matter Movement 48–50
Black women 4, 44–52; police killings of 44, 45–47
Brodie, N. 83
Brown, Melissa 48

Chao, Anne 39n14
Chasi, C. 89
children 13, 74, 75, 81, 82, 86–88, 112, 114, 120
civilian casualties 33
code of honor, Africa 81–91
conflict 2, 3, 8–11, 19, 20, 22–26, 30, 32, 33, 35, 36, 39, 66; transformation 24, 25
conflict-related sexual violence (CRSV) 8, 10, 11; survivors 9–12
convictions 25, 60, 66
Corradi, C. 84
country-level definition 5, 94, 97–99
Covid-19 5, 6, 56, 59, 64, 125, 127–129, 131
Crenshaw, Kimberlé 45, 47, 51, 52
crimes 14, 15, 21–23, 25, 27, 34, 60, 64, 67, 81, 82, 95, 96
criminal justice system 25, 47, 51, 55, 56, 59–61, 66, 67
Cullen, P. 84
cultural violence 130, 131

Dawkins, Sophia 32n6
Diallo, Y. 86, 90
dictatorships 19, 20, 24–26
D'Ignazio, Catherine 31n3

direct violence 95, 130, 131
domestic violence 2, 8, 13, 59, 62, 71, 78, 129, 131
Domestic Violence Act 61, 64
Dzhanova, Yelena 46

education 12, 117, 119, 122, 131

face-to-face conversation 57
families 9, 10, 13, 55, 62, 71, 72, 77, 78, 81, 82, 88, 116–118; femicide 55, 62; homicides 60
female circumcision 73–76, 78
female genital mutilation 4, 35, 72–76
female homicide 37, 129
femicidal violence 31, 35, 36, 38, 131
femigenocide 35
firearms 59, 65
Foucault, Michael 14

García-Del Moral, Paulina 84
gender inequalities 22, 95, 108
gender-based femicide 60
gender-based violence (GBV) 3, 8, 9, 12, 14, 15, 18, 61, 81, 82, 85, 94–97, 107, 120, 121, 126
gendered violence 8, 21, 51
genital mutilation 61, 72, 73, 129
genocidal femicide 114
genocide 5, 22, 23, 112–123; survivors 116–123
Gilbert, Keon 46
global scourge 83–85
global security 21–24
Guatemalan conflict 35
Gutiérrez-Sanín, Francisco 35–36

harmful practices 71–73, 78
Henrik, Belfrage 64
honor killings 3, 4, 62, 71–73, 76–78
human dignity 85, 86
human insecurity 18, 19, 24, 26

Ibrahim, Habiba 46
imam 74, 76

informed socio-ecological model 99–100
international legal instruments 4, 81, 82, 90
intersectional invisibility approach 49
intersectionality 45, 50
intimate partner femicide (IPF) 4, 56, 58, 59, 62, 64, 65, 84, 96
intimate partner violence 8, 11–13, 129
invisible police lethal violence 44–52
Iranzo, Juan Manuel 54

Jewkes, R. 84
Jill, Radford 60
Johnson, Odis 46

Kateb, G. 86
Kelly, Liz 18
King, Ruth 39n14
Klein, Lauren F. 31n3
Krause, S. R. 86

Lagarde y de los Ríos, Marcela 30n1
lethal violence 22, 35, 37, 39, 84
López, Geofredo Angulo 64

male homicides 60, 95, 129
Mathews, S. 84
measurement challenges 30, 35
media coverage 4, 47, 96
medical model 127, 128
medical suicide 126, 127
Méndez, Crippa 66
mental illness 46, 126–128
misogynist motivation 60
missingness 31, 38
Mugumbate, J. 89
multiple datasets 38
multiple systems estimation (MSE) 38, 39
Musila, G. A. 83

national femicide prevention strategy 101, **104–106**, 107
national integrated strategy 97–107
North Caucasus 4, 71–76, 78
Nwolise, O. 87, 88
Nyanguru, A. 89

operational ambiguities 33
operationalizations 34, 37

patriarchal societies 55, 64
police stations 9, 11, 13, 15, 64
police violence 4, 44–52
political femicide 4, 57, 62, 66
political violence 57
potential interventions 67–68

prevention strategy 4, 94, 97, 107
Price, Megan 39n14
psychological violence 15, 71, 72
public health problem 95

quantitative analyses 33, 36, 40

Radford, Jill 30n1, 54
Reardon, Betty 19
religious organizations 71, 74, 79
reparations response 9–11
reporting biases 33
reproductive violence 72
risk assessment tool 107
Rozo Ángel, Valentina 33n8
Russell, Diana E. H. 30n1, 34, 60, 61
Rwandan genocide 5, 112–114, 123
Rwandan society 123

Say Her Name Campaign 50–51
secondary victimization 10–13
self-destruction 125
sexism 44, 45, 49, 51, 61, 130
sexual and gender-based violence (SGBV) 3, 7–15, 18, 25, 26
Sexual Offenses Act 61
sexual violence 5, 9–12, 22, 23, 25, 30, 35, 37
shadow pandemic 59, 62, 129
shame 55, 62, 77, 118
Sigsworth, Romi 24
social facts 125, 131, 132
social model 6, 127, 128, 131
social values 85, 87, 88
South Africa 67, 68, 82, 83, 94–101
Standish, Katerina 55
state violence 47, 52
state-sponsored femicide 66
statistical biases 30, 32, 33, 38
statistical patterns 31, 39
stigmatization 11, 32, 120
stranger femicides 56, 58, 65
structural violence 8, 9, 11–13, 15
suicidal violence 6, 126–128, 132
suicide 2, 6, 9, 68, 125–128, 131, 132
Swaine, Aisling 25

tactical sexual violence 9
Tavera Fenollosa, Ligia 38n13
theory of change 100
traditional femicide 73, 78
transformative justice 24–27
transitional justice 24–26, 112
trauma counseling 117
Tripp, Aili Mari 21
Tutsi women 5, 113–115, 123
Tutsis 5, 112–114, 117, 119, 123

INDEX

Ubuntu 4, 85, 86, 88–91

Valji, Nahla 24
victimization 10, 11, 40, 97; Kosovo 7–15
victims 13, 14, 31–34, 37, 39, 47, 57, 60, 62, 64, 81, 125
violence 2, 8, 9, 18, 19, 24, 26, 31, 32, 35–38, 54, 66, 82, 125, 129–131; patterns of 31, 34, 37–39
violence against women (VAW) 18–20, 23–25, 27, 126

Walby, Sylvia 36, 37
weapons of war 62, 66
Weil, Shalva 55, 62, 83
women: killing of 2, 4, 25, 55, 61, 129, 130; protection of 81, 83, 85–90; survivors 112–124
Wood, Elisabeth Jean 35, 36

Zimbabwe 4, 54–57, 59, 61, 62, 64–68
Zimbabwe Human Rights Commission 57